ACHIEVING ISN'T EVERYTHING
It's the Only Thing

Bill Welp
Don Scott

Produced and printed by: Fred Weidner & Son Printers, Inc., New York
Cover design and design consultants: Communigraphics, New York

Library of Congress Card Catalog Number 81-90679
ISBN 0-9607708-0-1

TABLE OF CONTENTS

process of O.P.E.N. What happens when we use O.P.E.N. Misconceptions about the process of O.P.E.N. What O.P.E.N. is and is not. How to apply O.P.E.N. to achieve what you want.

A detailed development of the communication process. How O/C controls that process. Identification of the major blocks to reaching understanding and agreement. How O/C overcomes those blocks. The dynamics of human interaction. How what you do affects me and vice-versa. Methods and approach to self-understanding ... the three-sided personality. Identification of the human needs present in all of us. The importance of value. How to identify value in dealing with other people.

Why objective setting is so difficult. Problems with identifying our own needs. Reasons for poor objective setting. What happens when objectives are not clearly thought out. The process of establishing meaningful objectives.

INTRODUCTION

Jim said to Frank: "I'll meet you at the Chrysler corner at 42nd St. and Third Avenue, at 4:00 on Friday." Jim just did something that no other being on earth but a human can do. If Frank heard him and understood, Jim communicated.

We as humans have been accorded a rare gift — the capability of communicating with each other. We don't have to go beyond the Tower of Babel story to understand the importance of being able to communicate. From the smallest projects, to the World Trade Center, to the supersonic, to walking on the moon, to the satellites, to the variety of food we eat, our health, the clothes we wear, and on and on — all are made possible because we can communicate.

Communication is a great gift. What a shame we often do more harm with it than good!

We assume that we communicate. We assume that all we have to do is to say something or write something and our receiver now fully understands the message. And nothing could be further from the truth.

The *Harvard Business Review*, back in the mid '50's, revealed a comprehensive research program that concluded that communication among business executives was less than 40% effective. A rule of thumb for retention of any information heard at a lecture puts it at less than 25%. People are too busy trying to sort out the words to concentrate on understanding.

Think back for a minute to some antagonisms within your own family group. Weren't they generally the result of faulty communication? One side simply didn't understand the other.

Even troublesome dichotomies can be bridged with proper communication. But the impediments are numerous, and that's what this book is all about.

If we understand the impediments and wipe them out of our own communication, we become very powerful people. We control situations effectively — notice I said "situations," not other people. We can attain any reasonable objective. We can live our chosen life style. We can enjoy more friends than we have time for, and life can be just plain fun.

The poor animals are stuck with their lot. There's no hope of changing it. But we, as people, have the whole world open to us, and the key to that world is COMMUNICATION.

In these pages, we'll look at how *effective communication* can be easy, and why we make it so difficult. If somebody from another planet with the ability to understand were to creep up surreptitiously on two earthlings discussing a subject, the extra-terrestrial listener would hardly believe that these people could actually ever accomplish anything.

How we have taken a skill with the intrinsic capability of creating harmony and understanding between at least two people and converted it into our own little, selfishly-covered realm is mind-boggling. Instead of using communication to expand our relationships and well-being, we use it as an ever-diminishing protective device. It's almost as if, as we grow older, we grow mentally smaller.

O.K., sports fans, let's dissolve the cocoon. Let's open the way to richer, happier times, to delightful relationships, to a power we never could have believed possible. How to do it is all in the following pages.

By reading this book, and practicing the tenets in it you can not only open your own life, but make a better life for the people with whom you come in contact. That ought to be worthwhile.

1
WHY WE DON'T COMMUNICATE EFFECTIVELY

Let's put it right up front.

Mary Dillon is the new Vice President of Marketing for a medium-size fabric manufacturing company. Joe Babcock is Sales Manager and now reports to Mary. At 48, Joe's been around awhile, sixteen years to be exact. He coveted the job of Marketing Vice President, but really didn't expect to get it. He didn't expect Mary to get it, either.

Let's examine what's in each of their minds before they officially meet just after the announcement.

Mary reasons as follows:

"I've now got the big job. I'll bet a lot of the men around here are surprised to see a woman come along as I have. They're probably all set to test me. I'll lay odds they would like to see me foul up. They've a surprise in store. I've got my first meeting this morning with Joe Babcock, and I've done my homework.

"Joe thinks he understands his job. Wait until he finds out how much more I already know than he does. I might just as well set the record straight going in, because it's a cinch I won't attain my goals without their respect. I've got to show them I can play a man's game."

Now let's see what's going on in Joe's head:

"Oh, brother! I never thought I'd be in this position. There is no way that female can understand what goes on in this man's game. Unfortunately, she's the boss. I suppose the best thing to do is to let her yak and then go ahead and do it like I've always done it. After all, I didn't get this job because I was a total loss, but I do think I've got to let her know at the outset that I'm not going to be pushed around. I'll lay some of our field problems on her and watch her squirm. Well, it's five of nine—here goes!"

You've just seen a 24-carat example of one reason why we fracture the communication process. Neither of these people is going into that meeting with productive objectives. They're both going in with preconceived ideas, mind-sets (we'll talk more about this later) that will ultimately lead to psychological wounds that won't heal easily.

Let's look at another example.

Dad lent Johnny the car. One of the conditions was that Johnny would be home by 11:30 p.m. It's now midnight and Johnny isn't home, and Dad is fuming. Let's look at Dad's thoughts.

"I'm going to blast that kid before he gets in the door. He'll get that car again over my dead body! I don't know what flimsy excuse he's going to put up, but he's got to learn that when I say 11:30, I mean 11:30."

Let's see what's going on in Johnny's mind, as he stands on the side of the parkway, waiting for the police to come by. His car ran out of gas an hour ago:

"Gee, I never thought to look at the gas gauge. Why does my father always let the gas run down to the bottom before he fills it up? I can see the old goat now, raging up and down the living room. He's not going to give me a chance to say a word. O.K., he can take his car and stuff it."

These are simply two examples of why we don't communicate. Our minds are made up going in. Sometimes the mind-set is not quite as emotionally charged, but if it is set at all, it is damaging to the understanding process.

Think back in your own recent past. Think of the communication instances in which you have been involved. How many times have you gone in with your mind made up:

1. with pre-judgment of your listener and his possible reaction.

2. with a message you were going to force across, regardless.

3. with how you were going to counteract anything he or she said.

4. with only your own specific objectives in mind.

Most of our communication, because of mind-set and other emotions, is sabotaged before we start. We enter a self-protective win/lose situation. "Somebody's going to walk away with the loaf, and that somebody's going to be 'me.'"

Let's pick a figure out of the air ... it won't be far off. Ninety percent of all our communication attempts are not thought out beforehand, are not pre-structured, and are, therefore, based on our own mind-set. We are playing "communication roulette" every time we face a human interaction. We run around with a word shovel, digging holes for ourselves.

Like paranoia, the disease feeds on itself. We build the cocoon thicker and dare anyone to try to come in. Unfortunately, the thing we are protecting has no value, not even to ourselves. There is no market for our own prejudice. Nobody wants even to listen to the reason behind it, yet we protect it with everything we've got. We pride ourselves on our ability to come away from a communications encounter with a "win." No one ever stops to assess the value, the tremendous value, of having your *listener* go away with a win. Does it occur to us that if we ever established the reputation for having our listeners walk away with a "win," everyone in our community would vie for the opportunity to communicate with us, to get to know us, to elect us to public office, to value our friendship, to talk with us about how to spend their money? Apparently not. That is why there is always a war going on, why many executive positions in corporations are filled with incompetents.

Emotions Are Both Wonderful and Dangerous

In one sense, emotions are magic. They are the basis for compassion without which we would be animals. They are a protective device. They are the basis for love and affection, for raising good children, for assuring valued and long-range relationships.

It is unfortunate that they can also, as in the above example, muddle the communication process, often beyond repair.

They range from love to hate, from glee to despair. Throughout our lives they cause us to commit acts that are embarassing and sometimes degrading. They make it easy for us to say things which are meaningless, misleading, maddening and expensive.

The industrial psychologist Maslow says that the psychological needs of man are even more important to him than the "will to survive." A child's first organized thoughts are based on the need to be recognized as an individual. "Daddy, look at me!," "Mommy, see what I drew." We mature, but the need to be recognized never leaves us. And Maslow says something else: the need is insatiable. How successful we would be as communicators if we used that bit of information in dealing with others, but controlled the need in ourselves.

The key is control. Control your own emotions for a major step in eliminating communication problems.

Notice, we did not say "eliminate," for emotion exists in all of us. It cannot be legislated out of existence. But if we control it in ourselves, that will clarify our mind-set and we can objectively search for win/win. When we control our own emotion, that can help defuse the destructive emotion in others.

As damaging as emotions can be in the communication process, they are just the start of the problem. Even if we eliminate mind-set and preconceived convictions, and attempt to enter the communication process with an open mind, there are countless other obstacles to good communication.

So far most of the work done to cure the disease of poor communication has centered around the skills of communication. The massive effort has been to correct the problem by improving people's *skills*: listening skills, non-verbal communication skills, the use and meaning of words, etc. The basic *process* of communication against which these separate skills are applied has not been defined and structured. The result is that people have a lot of tools but no unifying process which tells them *when* to use a particular skill... or *how* that skill should interface with the rest.

It is similar to bringing a team of specialists together to create a vehicle capable of carrying objects through the air. The separate skills (disciplines) could be metallurgy, electronics, computer processing of information, hydraulics, propulsion, etc.

These disciplines will never be able to interact together effectively to create a product which will fly, without the underlying structure and discipline of *aerodynamics*. Without that underlying structure, which ties all of the disciplines together, nothing will ever be created that works.

The same is true with communication. The structure of communication is like the structure of aerodynamics in the analogy. Each of the separate disciplines — listening, feedback, non-verbal communication, etc. — can be integrated into a meaningful approach which accomplishes the purpose of all communication ... meaningful interaction between people.

Webster's Dictionary defines communication as *"the process by which meanings are exchanged between individuals through a common system of symbols."* The first key word is *process*—that is, the structure which enables people to interact and exchange *meanings*.

If the process is understood by people, then they have the method by which they can interact. With this common structure, the complex process of exchanging meanings can take place. Without a common structure, the result can be chaos.

Most of our formal education has not provided any understanding of the structure of communication. We are taught separate disciplines for using the senses (sight, hearing, touch) in order to receive and send messages. The result is that we are mostly sloppy, undisciplined communicators.

Here is a real-life example which should hit home. Test yourself in this situation:

> Ted Brown is the General Manager of a large division of a major corporation, Acme, Inc. He is about to start a staff meeting. His department managers know that the division has been successful for the last two years. They have racked up increases in profits, volume and return on assets managed. They also know that it was costly in terms of long hours of work and hard decisions about marginal employees. The organization was pushed to its very limit to achieve the objectives.

> Here are the opening comments of Ted Brown:

> "Gentlemen, you have received the cost, volume and profit objectives for this division for the next year. It is obvious that the corporation is asking a lot of this division. We need some hard-nosed discussion of this financial plan. How do you feel it will affect your department operations?"

Did you understand Ted Brown to say, "I want your individual plans and personal commitment now"?

Or did you understand, "Let's get all the problems out on the table so that we can address them *as a team* and find the answers to these problems"?

Or did you understand, "I need some facts and support from you to be able to go back to corporate and prove that the numbers are unrealistic and unattainable"?

It is obvious that the three interpretations would result in tremendously different actions on the part of the department managers.

If you picked any of the above, you fell into the trap of being an undisciplined listener...as assumer and a reactor.

Ted Brown did not clearly communicate:

1. What response he was looking for.
2. How he felt about the subject personally.
3. The type of attitude that he wanted to see from the department managers.

He had done what so many of us do. He had not prepared effectively for this communication, and most importantly, he had set the stage for numerous types of interpretations of that communication. This is a sure way to damage the relationship between people.

In the actual case, all three of the interpretations listed were made by the department managers. The result was confusion, then anger. Ted Brown finally said, "Dammit, that's one of our major problems. You guys just don't try to understand."

Is this an isolated example? Absolutely not! Dr. Don Kirkpatrick of the University of Wisconsin indicates that two out of three of the mistakes that occur in business organizations are the result of poor communication. Someone did not understand a directive, an intent, a fact, an idea, an assumption. The result was an incorrect action or no action at all when it was vitally important to act.

The *Productivity Center* headquartered in Houston, Texas, estimates that the cost of mistakes due to misunderstanding runs anywhere from ten to thirty-five percent of the gross revenues of a business organization. And mistakes are only the tip of the cost iceberg.

Here's another example of the problem and its cost:

The ABC Company has a large manufacturing unit producing a control process for a specific military aircraft. Cal Corbett is Plant Superintendent. Suddenly, and without warning, this particular plane is made obsolete by a defense department edict. The ABC execs are delighted. They can now turn their energy and production capacity to more profitable commercial endeavors.

Important to their plan is holding on to the skilled labor under Cal. Cal knows this. Unfortunately, Cal assumes that his people understand what an opportunity this is. Rather than giving them promises, he decides to wait to communicate with them until he has something specific to say. He thinks that will really do the trick.

By the time management noticed the egress, the feelers and résumés were out, and ABC had lost half of its skilled personnel. The cost of poor communication... millions!

Thus we can see that poor communication is not just a problem... it is a disease. It's a disease because it matches the dictionary definition of a disease down to a tee... "An impairment of the normal state of the living organism that affects the performance of its vital function." That's exactly what poor communication is. It stops the normal functioning of an organization. Instead of people interacting positively together to accomplish a return for their mutual investment in time, energy and effort, their energies are dissipated or spent against each other in misunderstanding and mistrust. Thus the performance of the vital functions of the organization is impaired if not seriously injured.

The Cost to You Personally of Poor Communication

For individuals, poor communication can be agonizing and painful.

Listen to these statements. See if they don't sound familiar.

"That's your problem. You just don't try to understand. You're so interested in making your own point that you don't listen to me."

"You're playing games. Reaching conclusions which simply don't exist."

"I don't understand why you get so defensive every time we talk."

"Okay, you've made your point, but don't think that's going to change anything."

These statements are a direct reflection of poor communication in our personal lives. The emotional cost is staggering. Feelings are deeply hurt. Relationships become cold and indifferent. Friends are lost. Parents and children lose respect for each other. Marriages get into serious trouble. Self-esteem goes down the drain. Anxieties and frustrations fester and grow.

One of the major reasons is the lack of or a poorly defined philosophy.

The dictionary defines philosophy as "the beliefs, attitudes and values of an individual." Our philosophy is our internal guidance system. It controls our actions. It controls how we respond to other people. It tells us whether or not to become involved with someone. It tells us what we believe is moral and ethical.

If this guidance system is based on the belief that all people are selfish and will only act to better themselves, then we had better defend ourselves. We had better use a system of communication which will enable us to control others. If we don't control them, they will control us.

There's another philosophy or internal guidance system which says that people have to live together in the future. That both persons can receive what they need without either person being deprived. That there can be a balance of power. This is what we call a win/win philosophy.

There are the two philosophical extremes. One is a win/win philosophy, the other a win/lose philosophy. Between these two there is a long continuum...a great gray area where most of us live. Because of that gray area, we do not have an internal guidance system which we use with any consistency. The result is confusion and distrust.

What another person sees and hears is your actions and words. If they do not reflect a consistent philosophy, they telegraph that you are not being totally honest.

The lack of a consistent philosophy, not manipulation, is the major problem in communication. The undisciplined communicator ends up with a "poor communication" ... a communication which does not accomplish its goal ... a communication which is easily, and usually, misread.

Remember, our dictionary definition of communication is "the process by which *meanings* are exchanged." Meanings are evidences of our values, of our internal guidance systems. Because most people do not consistently demonstrate either a win/win or a win/lose philosophy, there is confusion. People do not understand the intent or the meanings of others. They become defensive. They say things in their own defense which hurt others. This leads to misunderstanding and distrust. The result can be anything from a minor error to a major catastrophe.

When an individual doesn't have a consciously thought out philosophy and doesn't have a structure to insure that the process of communication is occurring, the result normally is lose/lose.

Let's look at what happens to us as we grow. The naive, unstructured approach is a wonderful thing to watch in a child. In adult communication, it's pure disaster. As we grow up, we start to run into trouble with our naivete. We assume simplicity and honesty in all relationships. The result is that we are taken advantage of. We then become at least a little cynical and jaded. We start to believe that everyone is selfish, that we had better look out for Number One. The result is that we develop communication habits which are manipulative.

Here's the fascinating part of this scenario: Once we act in a manipulative way, our actions are immediately read by others as being closed. Now they react in a similar way. And their reaction proves to us that we were right. People really are selfish. Even those very close to us.

Remember the old song, "You Always Hurt the One You Love." The reason for the hurt, unstructured communication...

Words... Symbols of Understanding... Symptoms of the Disease of Poor Communication

Ninety percent of our communication is verbal, or with words, yet only 8% of our total knowledge came to us through the ear. This tells us something rather startling.

All the words we throw around are not really doing much of a communication job. The semanticists found this out a long time ago. The word *semantics* comes from the Greek word *semantikos*, which means the significance of signs and symbols, and implies "the effect on our thinking of signs and symbols."

The same sign or symbol can connote entirely different things to different people. A cocktail glass might suggest an exciting glamorous party to one person, while it may remind another of a hangover.

The concept of *Levels of Abstraction* (see pg. 13) helps us understand how these different connotations can affect our communication.

A *word* is not the *"Real Thing,"* and what this means in our communication is emphasized by the psychologist's concept of *individual differences.*

People are just as different as fingerprints. Their parents, background, education, friends, hangouts, etc. all differ. The product is therefore different. So we find ourselves trying to communicate with obscure and often distant *levels of abstraction* with people who are as different from us as turtles from birds.

Unfortunately, each of us is limited by his or her own experiences. There is no way we can think beyond them. That's why the Rorschach test works. After all, it's just a series of semantical ink blots. Nobody drew them; they just came out that way. When any one of us looks at an ink blot, it can only remind us of what's already in our minds. If we look at enough of them, what we see reveals a mind-set to the trained psychologist or psychiatrist.

Words are symbols and therefore are similar to ink blots. Of themselves, they often carry countless meanings. The word "face" in the English language has 26 meanings. The word "check" in the English language has 29 meanings. Ask five of your friends to define the word "sophisticated." You'll get some funny definitions, very few of which will come anywhere close to the dictionary definition, because the word "sophisticated" comes from the Greek "sophist." The Sophists were people who roamed the countryside expounding philosophies which sounded reasonable but were often self-serving and false. The true meaning of "sophisticated" is a "veneer," or "not the real thing."

There are many who "parade" words. They use them to impress, not to express. And this is not funny.

For example, the following letter from the Veterans Administration didn't mean a thing to its addressee:

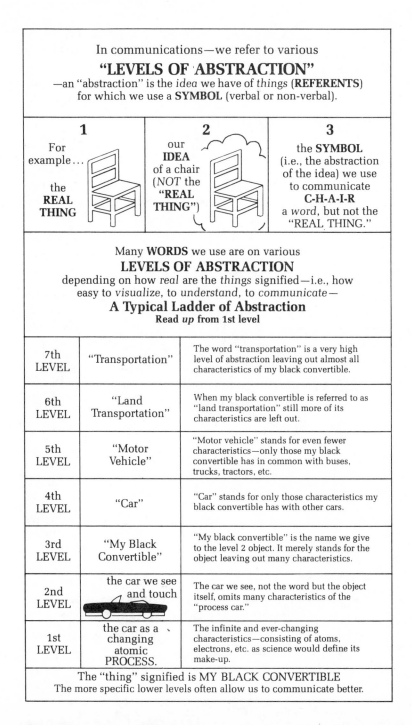

In communications—we refer to various
"LEVELS OF ABSTRACTION"
—an "abstraction" is the *idea* we have of *things* (**REFERENTS**)
for which we use a **SYMBOL** (verbal or non-verbal).

1	**2**	**3**
For example... the **REAL THING**	our **IDEA** of a chair (*NOT* the "**REAL THING**")	the **SYMBOL** (i.e., the abstraction of the idea) we use to communicate **C-H-A-I-R** a *word*, but not the "REAL THING."

Many **WORDS** we use are on various
LEVELS OF ABSTRACTION
depending on how *real* are the *things* signified—i.e., how
easy to *visualize*, to *understand*, to *communicate*—
A Typical Ladder of Abstraction
Read *up* from 1st level

7th LEVEL	"Transportation"	The word "transportation" is a very high level of abstraction leaving out almost all characteristics of my black convertible.
6th LEVEL	"Land Transportation"	When my black convertible is referred to as "land transportation" still more of its characteristics are left out.
5th LEVEL	"Motor Vehicle"	"Motor vehicle" stands for even fewer characteristics—only those my black convertible has in common with buses, trucks, tractors, etc.
4th LEVEL	"Car"	"Car" stands for only those characteristics my black convertible has with other cars.
3rd LEVEL	"My Black Convertible"	"My black convertible" is the name we give to the level 2 object. It merely stands for the object leaving out many characteristics.
2nd LEVEL	the car we see and touch	The car we see, not the word but the object itself, omits many characteristics of the "process car."
1st LEVEL	the car as a changing atomic PROCESS.	The infinite and ever-changing characteristics—consisting of atoms, electrons, etc. as science would define its make-up.

The "thing" signified is MY BLACK CONVERTIBLE
The more specific lower levels often allow us to communicate better.

"The non-compensable evaluation heretofore assigned you for your service-connected disability is confirmed and continued."

The veterans who got this information wrote back: "What the hell does this mean?"

The writer would never have dreamed of saying, "You ain't sick, so you ain't gonna get paid." Yet the second version would have been understood.

The chairman of a large food company was doing a plant tour with the president and a consultant. The consultant was trying to look bright. He said, "My, you have a plethora of merchandise." The chairman turned to the president and asked, "What did he say?" From the president: "We're up to our asses in cans."

We laugh. But one communicated, the other didn't. Rudolph Flesch wrote:

"Vocabulary building as a major industry dates back to some intelligence tests that were given to various occupational groups about a dozen years ago. It turned out that big executives topped everybody else in the range of their vocabulary. That's not a particularly exciting discovery since corporation officials usually get to be where they are after they have had a lot of diversified experience. But the vocabulary builders have seized upon that little experiment and quoted it in hundreds of full page ads since. Their logic is simple: Top executives have top vocabulary; hence, vocabulary means success. And so the battle cry was born: 'Build up your vocabulary for quick advancement.'

"The other day I glanced through one of the best known of the vocabulary-building books. The preface explained proudly that after studying the book the reader wouldn't say 'He was as busy as a bee' anymore but 'He was bustling and industrious.' Exactly. He would get ashamed of his natural idioms and pepper his speech and writing with strained and ill-fitting expressions.

"In another book I found the word to 'brachiate' among those to be studied. The definition was to swing by your arms from the branches of a tree like a monkey. Which reminded me of the wise old lady's rule to 'keep away from fancy words because you never can tell what they mean.'"

We are not saying, "Don't improve your vocabulary." By all means work at getting as erudite as you can with the time you have.

But don't lose track of the objective, which is to "communicate." In exchanging meanings, words are only the symbols we use. Our experience tells us what the symbols mean. The real definition of words is not in the dictionary, but in people.

Inflection, Another Monkey Wrench

Words are only part of the verbal problem.

Look at the following sentence:

"How can you say that?"

Sentence? *One* sentence? There are at least five of them there. Go over the sentence and emphasize a different word each time. In each case the meaning changes totally.

Inflection enters the scenario. We start to communicate with words which didn't mean much in the first place, add inflection, and we emerge with a hodgepodge that in no way communicates. As a matter of fact, the Chinese have as many as nine different inflections on one word — and each inflection changes the meaning of the word entirely. That's why the Chinese have trouble communicating from one province to another.

To sum up: we have a thought of our own, based on our own experience, our own mind-set. We throw out a feeble ink blot (words) which is subject to the interpretation of our listener and his or her own experience and his or her own mind-set.

To clear up the potential muddle, what we need is a *structure* which insures that the blocks to communication can be identified *and* controlled. Again, we are back to *structure* ... the framework which will pinpoint and control the areas where communication can go astray.

Helen Keller's life is a beautiful example of the importance of *structuring* the communication process. The movie about her life starts with scenes of a young girl reacting violently to everybody around her. She strikes out ... pulls back defensively ... searches for affection ... slaps at attempts to reach her.

Without the capacity to see or hear, she has no way to communicate. She can't hear herself think, so she can't verbalize ... can't even conceive of how to communicate with others. The world is hostile, unpredictable, full of awful surprises. She strikes out at those attempting to love her. She is one step above an animal ... NO ... one step below! She can't see or hear, and has not developed any structure for relating to others.

There is no *structure* by which she can interact. No vehicle of communication has been established. There is no understanding of the intent and meanings of either this young girl or other people. Meanings cannot be exchanged because there is no process, no structure.

The movie then shows a dedicated teacher, who after hundreds of unsuccessful attempts, finally establishes the *structure* by which this young girl can communicate effectively with others. She accomplishes this by using the only major sensory capacity she has ... touch. The structure of communication started with the pressure of the finger on the palm of her hand. The scene by the well where Helen recognizes that she has the capacity to communicate is the most moving part of the film. She now has the vehicle to understand love, to share experiences ... to live in the wonderful world of other people.

Now her parents had to be taught the same *structure* for communicating with Helen Keller. *Both* persons had to use the structure for communication to happen. It seems almost ludicrous, but the problem with most of us is that we came into the world with all of our senses. We have a tremendous capacity to interact with other people. We use all our senses, so if one is a little off, we support it with another. With this unbelievable capacity to communicate, to use all of our senses, we started assuming that others understood the *structure*. "I can talk and you can hear...so we must be communicating." Oh, how naive and wrong that is!

Let's go back to the simple meaning of *words*. With Helen Keller, each pattern of pressure on the palm meant one and only one thing. With us, each word could mean as many as a dozen things. How the word is said could lead to another seven interpretations.

Now we compound the problem by *assuming* that everybody knows how to *listen*, knows how to receive the true meaning and feeling of the broadcasted word. After all, *listening* is a natural skill! *No! Hearing* is a natural sensory capacity! *Listening* requires a lot more. First, it requires a structure ... a structure which insures *understanding* of the symbols we use to broadcast, and a double check on whether the receiver used the same interpretations.

It is a wonder that we can live together at all. Somewhere behind our relationship there must be a commonality, an "open sesame" that somehow keeps everything glued together.

So let's glue! In the following chapters, a successful approach to effective communication is fully explained. And it works!

2
THE ANSWER...O.P.E.N. COMMUNICATION

By now, communication must appear loaded with ogres. The obstacles loom larger than any chance of success. Maybe you're even beginning to wonder why we bother trying. We have made up our minds, listeners have made up theirs. The tools (words) we use most cause more problems than they solve. Where do we go from here?

There is a way.

Suppose we could put together a formula:

a.   where everyone came out a winner.

b.   that allayed any suspicion of skullduggery.

c.   that keeps power in balance, while

d.   getting a positive mind-set from the listener.

It almost seems like some form of mysticism, doesn't it ...as if maybe you have to learn hypnotism or feed somebody a drug or something. But it's not that difficult. There is a structure *and* a philosophy — easy to learn and to understand—that will help you to do just about anything you want to do with communication. It has a name...

O.P.E.N. Communication

The goal of O.P.E.N. Communication is Utopian — win/win. In any win/win situation, each side enjoys the trust of the other. Let's look at an example.

Let's go back to the situation of the General Manager of the division which was described in the first chapter. Remember the situation.

> The General Manager of a large division of a major corporation is about to start a staff meeting. He and his department managers know that the division has been very successful in the last two years. They have racked up increases in profits, volume, and return on assets managed. They also know that this was costly in terms of long hours of work and hard decisions about marginal employees. The organization was pushed to its very limit to achieve the objectives.

Hear now the O.P.E.N. Communication approach of the General Manager as he starts this staff meeting:

> "Gentlemen, our role as the management team of this division is to achieve the growth and profit objectives set by the corporation. I think I understand your concerns and fears. We have just pushed the hell out of the organization to accomplish the goals of last year. Can we justifiably do it again?
>
> "The objective of this meeting is to start the process of creating the department plans which will enable us to achieve this year's objectives. In the process of accomplishing these plans, we'll all grow in our capacity as professional managers. We'll prove to the corporation, our employees, and our customers that we are qualified to be the #1 company in this industry.
>
> "Now, here's the plan that I'd like to follow today to enable us to come to grips with the situation and find realistic answers."

If you were a department manager, sitting at that meeting, listening to that opener, the chances are your feelings would be positive. There would be no misunderstanding of the intent of the General Manager, of what was expected of you, of how the General Manager felt about the situation, and of what needs of yours would be met by actively participating in and accomplishing the objectives of the meeting.

Let's analyze what the General Manager did with that opening statement:

First, he dealt with the feelings and expectations of each one of the managers by stating, "I believe I understand your concerns and fears. We just pushed the hell out of the organization to accomplish the goals of last year. Can we justifiably do it again?"

By openly referring to the thoughts, feelings and experiences of his department managers, he is indicating a willingness to deal with these feelings. He is also indicating that he's not naive or attempting to ignore or push under the table the concerns of each individual.

Secondly, there should be no doubt in anybody's mind as to what the *objective* of the meeting is. Again, let's listen to the actual statement. "The objective of this meeting is to start the process of creating the individual department plans which will enable each one of us to achieve this year's (profit) objectives." Each department manager, therefore, knows that action is going to be required of him or her, both during the meeting and at the end of the meeting.

In addition, the manager dealt with the *needs* of each one of his department heads. "We'll all grow in our capacity as professional managers. We'll prove to the corporation, our employees and our customers that we are qualified to be the #1 company in this industry."

Each of the department managers will have to work hard and stick his or her neck out in order to accomplish the division's objectives. Why should they do it? They should because, as professionals, they need to grow in their capacity as managers. They have the need to prove to the corporation, to their own employees, and to their customers that they are the most professional managers in the industry.

The last element of the introduction was to let each manager see the *plan* that the General Manager had developed for use as a team to accomplish the objective for the meeting.

So there we have it. It wasn't just a glib introduction given by a con artist. It was a highly purposeful introduction which proved that the manager understood and was using the powerful O.P.E.N. Communication method.

The O.P.E.N. Communication structure demands that four elements be prepared for and addressed in every interaction between people. Let's go back and identify those four elements.

"O" Stands for Objective

Your *objective* is the specific action you want the other person to take as a result of your meeting. Spell it out in detail, because this is the action which is going to satisfy *your needs*.

By stating this objective up front, the Manager eliminates misunderstanding not only of his objective, but of the feelings behind it.

It's a common human tendency to "sneak up" on your objective. Don't! Bring it right out! Allay any suspicions right at the start. Furtiveness is not fertile ground for win/win communication.

Most communications have a purpose. Spell out clearly in your own mind the action you want from the listener. If you don't determine in advance the specific desired action, you can't very well make it clear in the meeting. You are going to provide enough facts for the *listener* to evaluate the action so you had better know *what* action you are *both* evaluating.

By stating the objective up front, the manager is eliminating the possibility of misunderstanding...misunderstanding not just of the action which is required, but of the intent behind that action.

All people know and understand that most interactions are purposeful...that the reason for communicating is to move another person into action, either now or at some time in the future. Therefore, we had better determine in advance what specific action we want the other person to take. Otherwise, our needs will not be met. Secondly, we must let the other person know what action we're going to ask him or her to take at the end of our meeting so that there is no misunderstanding, and so that he or she can evaluate whether or not this is an appropriate action to take.

"P" Stands for Plan

The plan is the sequence of facts, thoughts, ideas and proofs which both individuals will follow. The plan becomes the road map which each of us will use in order to determine if it is logical to arrive at the objective. Most important in the process is proving to each one that this will be a win/win situation...a situation where the needs of both of us will be met.

"E" Stands for Expectations

The expectations are the *mind-sets*. When two people meet, they bring into their interaction their past experiences with the subject to be discussed, their experiences with each other as people, their feelings about their lives, and even experiences which have happened just before they walked into the room. Remember, the first major block to communication was our mind-set. If we do not deal with these feelings and experiences, they could become a block to understanding. The other person may assume we care little about his or her feelings. He or she may even suspect deceit. *Expectation* is really where each person stands. If we are callous to emotion and feelings in the course of communication, they become a threat.

"N" Stands for Need

There is no reason why another person will take a suggested action unless there is something in it for him or her.

In your preparation, determine the benefits to your listener if he or she accepts your suggested action. *Need* exists for both parties in a communication, and recognition of these *needs* makes the communication a win/win situation.

There we have the structure of O.P.E.N. COMMUNICATION...

O.—OBJECTIVE ... the specific action you want the other person to take. This satisfies your need.

P. — PLAN ... the sequence of thoughts, ideas and proofs you will both use to determine if this is a win/win situation.

E. — EXPECTATION ... the experiences of the individual which could cause a negative mind-set.

N.—NEED...the "what's in it for the other person"... the specific benefits he or she will get.

At this point, our understanding of O.P.E.N. Communication is not much more than listing the titles of four acts in a play.

O.P.E.N. Communication requires that the structure of O.P.E.N. be used in three phases of the communication:

1. As we *prepare* for any interaction where the intent is to be able to live with the person in the future.

2. In the *60-second opener* to that interaction...the first broadcast that we give to prove that we have done our preparation using O.P.E.N.

3. In the execution of the *plan* which we have developed during our preparation and communicated to the other person during the 60-second opener.

Let's now examine each one of the four steps of O.P.E.N. in greater detail.

The Objective

Be specific in what you are seeking. Ask yourself the old editorial questions:

What	action do I want?
Why	is that a reasonable action?
Where	will the action take place?
When	will the action take place?
Who	is involved in the action?
How	will the action take place?

You won't always have to supply answers to all these questions, but it's a good list for checking your thoroughness.

Here's an example of an ordinary situation which reveals how easy it is for objectives to become confused:

"I want George to agree with me."

"To agree to what?"

"Well, to agree to the fact that the American Cancer Society is a worthwhile endeavor."

"It has to be more than that. George can agree that it is a worthwhile endeavor but not do anything about it."

"All right, I can see that. I want George to make a donation to the American Cancer Society."

"That's fine, but you know, George could give ten cents."

It is easy to see that if you do not know the *specific action* that you want George to take, the chances are that your needs will not be met. Establish your objectives carefully, reasonably and objectively, taking into consideration the needs of your listener.

Also, if your objectives are not clear, there is danger that your communication will be worse than just a waste of time. The other person may develop an attitude or take a course of action which is either negative or incorrect.

The Plan

Your plan will outline the sequence of ideas, with substantiation, which you will use in the communication. Ask yourself if you have done your homework. Did you get the necessary facts to provide both sides with a win/win? Did you bolster your 60-second opener with enough hard facts to make your case clear without telling your listener more about the situation than he wants to know?

The plan always starts with the 60-second opener. This is the critical tie-in between the preparation phase and the execution phase.

The specific steps in the plan after the 60-second opener should have an underlying pattern. However, these specific action steps will vary considerably depending upon the purpose of the interaction.

The Expectations

Have you considered your listener's *expectations*? Where does he or she stand? In determining what your listener expects, you must be cautious. You can never be *sure* what anyone's expectations are. Past experience is, of course, a tip-off. Naturally, the better you know a person, the better you can judge his or her expectations.

As we prepare for any interaction, we must know that the other individual is not going to come into that interaction pure as the driven snow... a slate that has never been written on. As soon as we come face to face, the other person will bring into that interaction feelings, thoughts, ideas, expectancies based upon all of his or her previous experiences. As we prepare, we must think our way through what experiences the individual has had and is living through. This will determine what his or her mind-set, feelings, thoughts, and ideas will be as we come face to face. If we don't know that mind-set, it will act as a barrier.

The second part of the **E** for *expect* is to establish the specific roles that each of us will play during this interaction. This then establishes what each of us can expect from the other and also establishes the ground rules for this interaction.

For example, if the interaction is a *counselling session* between a manager and an assistant, then the expectation would be:

> "To lay out the ground rules, you can expect me to provide my experiences and background. I'll ask questions to make sure that you have thought your way through the consequences of the various actions that you can take.

> "You can also expect me not to give you the decision. We both know that this is totally your responsibility and authority. You must be free to make the decision that you want to make."

Let's look at an example of dealing with expectations:

Don Jones is President of Collingwood Publishing Company. He has his eye on an acquisition. He knows that if he swings this acquisition, there will be a period of rather high expense as the new company folds into the policies at Collingwood. The long-range profits, however, appear excellent.

At the same time, Don has wanted to dissolve the rather large Research Department of Collingwood. In recent years most of Collingwood's major research projects have been farmed out. Collingwood's department is really just doubling most of the effort.

The Chairman of Collingwood, Clem Fifer, was the company founder and regards the entire company rather paternally. The Research Department is one of his babies. He has bragged for years that the Research Department helped put Collingwood where it is. This is true, but times have changed.

Don sees his job as persuading the old man to give up a loser to gain a winner. At lunch, Don's approach goes as follows:

"Clem, I know that your Number One desire before you retire is to see Collingwood become one of the most respected publishing companies in the business. It would certainly be a testimonial to you. Practically everything we have around here you had a hand in building.

"It's only natural that you feel a bit fatherly toward this entire operation. Yet, so that we can take on the new acquisition and not suffer a loss of profits, I'm suggesting that we reduce the size of our Research Department. I would like to go through my plans for phasing out the operation so that no one will get hurt, and profits will be generated."

Notice what Don Jones did. He immediately brought into the open what he knew would be important concerns to his listener. He recognized the emotional barrier involved. He dealt with it by comparing it to the much more substantial gains to be made. He turned it into a win/win situation—no one would be hurt, everyone would win.

The result would be a positive mind-set on the part of the listener, because all possible negative mind-sets were dealt with up front.

1. He knew what was being asked.
2. His primary needs were being addressed.
3. His emotional involvement in the Research Department was addressed.
4. He knew that the manager had a plan that they would both go through to make sure it would be a win/win situation.

The Need

Now that you've identified (in your objectives) the specific course of action you want the other person to take, there's no earthly reason why that person should take it...unless there is something in it for him or her.

When people commit themselves to a course of action, they are paying a price. They are taking a risk. As we prepare for our interaction, we must know enough about the other person and the conditions under which he or she is now or will be living to identify what value that individual will receive when he or she takes the action we want taken.

Let's take an example.

Dave Banks has just been hired as Executive Vice President for the company. His boss, John Mills, seems a reasonable person, but Dave really doesn't know much about him. Pre-employment interviews always present parties in their best posture.

After two weeks on the job, Dave discovers several things about the company that he knows should be changed, and he feels he must make a presentation to John, but he really doesn't know where John stands. Are any of these changes John's sacred cows? Maybe John started some of these situations and might not want to admit they haven't worked out. Yet Dave feels a responsibility to suggest the changes, and faces John Mills' needs as follows:

Any good president wants a more successful company.

He wants higher productivity and lower costs.

He wants better relationships around the shop and wants a happier Board of Directors.

He wants to look good in the eyes of those above him, the Board, and those below him, the employees.

Let's look at Dave's first sixty seconds:

"John, when you brought me in, you made it clear that you wanted me to look at all the areas of our operation where we might improve productivity, lower costs and make higher profits. I would like to discuss some specific areas where those benefits can be obtained.

"I know you are presently preparing for a Board meeting where you probably will be pinned down on the profit situation. I have made a list of areas where, by making minimal changes, we could give you a pretty good story for the Board.

"Here's the list and the calculated savings. I believe they're pretty accurate. You won't have to be uneasy about accepting them.

"I'm fairly new, so if there are some things on this list that, for reasons I may not be familiar with, you don't want to tackle right now, let's discuss them."

Notice that Dave used the needs area very effectively. He gave John sound reasons why any president would want to go ahead with changes that would provide those benefits.

He also gave John a way out. Dave banked on a win/win situation, i.e., if John is getting more out of making the changes than he gets by not going along with them, he will probably approve the changes.

Can the opener always be done in sixty seconds? Recognize the fact that the opener does not usually contain the whole story. Its purpose is to get the listener in the desired mind-set, one that says, "I'm willing to communicate objectively." Most times, you don't really need sixty seconds.

Look at an example of an O.P.E.N. Communicator using a five-second opener:

> Joe Garvin is driving his car along the Ventura Freeway in Southern California. The car in front of him stops suddenly and he has to slam on his brakes. The lady driving the Volvo behind Joe slams on her brakes, but, unfortunately, not quite in time. The front end of her car slides under Joe's bumper, smashing her grill, both fenders and her headlights. Instantly, the doors of both cars fly open, and Joe and the lady advance toward each other.

Joe is an O.P.E.N. Communicator. This is his (five second) thought process as they approach each other on the freeway:

1. OBJECTIVE.   To get the paperwork filled out so the accident can be reported as quickly as possible.

2. EXPECTATION.   Her mental state when we meet will obviously be very upset and irrational. She could blame the whole thing on me.

3. NEED.   Her need is really exactly the same as mine...to get the paperwork done and to get these cars towed away. Nothing else can be done now.

4. PLAN. What's my plan? It's a single one-step plan because here we are, face to face.

Five-Second Opener

JOE: "Ma'am, I'm sorry about this, and you must be upset. But the only thing we can do now is to get the paperwork filled out with the police."

Immediately, the woman, who is distraught, will interrupt, because there is no way that Joe's five-second opener will drain the emotion out of this situation. She will say things like: "My God, look at what you've done to my car!" "How could you be so stupid?" "Don't you know that this is a brand new car?" "Oh, my God, look at the front...what will my husband say?"

But Joe simply repeats his five-second opener, each time in a slightly different version: "(I think) I understand your concern, but the only thing we can do now is to get the paperwork filled out so this situation can be corrected."

Joe, in effect, lets the lady get the emotions out of her system until finally she recognizes that he is not attacking her. He is trying to arrive at a mutually beneficial conclusion. Eventually, she says, "Yes, I guess you're right. That's really all we can do."

In situations like this one, most people strike out defensively. They automatically put the blame on the other person, and the result is a confrontation that borders on war. This could result in the accident being reported improperly, so both parties would lose.

To repeat, the purpose of the opener is to establish a positive mind-set and atmosphere. Our objective is to communicate openly and accurately to arrive at decisions which will mutually benefit both of us...a win/win situation.

What is magic about *sixty seconds*? Behavioral scientists have learned that most people can listen for no more than sixty seconds before they feel the compulsion to say something...to interrupt. This would allow us a maximum of sixty seconds to establish a mind-set.

It has been a principle for years in the professional communication field of radio, TV, advertising, etc., that if something can be said in ten words, don't use twenty.

Some very interesting and complex objectives can be accomplished in sixty seconds. When you look at most commercials on TV, or hear them on the radio, sixty seconds is really the outside. Rarely does a commercial last more than half that time. When you stop to think that a product is described, its benefits extolled, and its value to the public explained, all within less than sixty seconds, you realize that sixty seconds is truly a luxurious space of time in which to set the mind.

Go through your communication plan to assure that you don't have more in what you plan to say than you need. Words can confuse. The more words, the more possibility for confusion. Therefore, it's always a good idea to plan your communication with an economy of words.

What we are asking you to do in the sixty-second opener is to go against a lifetime of training. It's as natural as the sun coming up for anyone to think of himself or herself first. It is a self-protective device. It's in all of us. Yet what we are asking you to do in these sixty seconds is to consider the mind-set of the emotions *and* needs of your listener.

This makes a lot of sense. In reality, if you don't do something about the mind-set of your listener, you'll be wasting your time, anyway. Let's look at an example of the kind of communication we see all the time when a sixty-second opener is not well planned.

Joe Barnett just returned from his three-week vacation from his job as Vice President of Sales for Consolidated. Joe was strolling through the warehouse the first morning and found a large shipment consigned to one of his big customers, Amalgamated Enterprises, standing in a corner of the warehouse. He called over the warehouse foreman and said, "Jim, what's that doing there? Looks to me like it's been there for over a week."

Jim says, "Well, Joe, we were all set to ship it out, and Cal Jones called in and said not to ship any more to Amalgamated."

Joe Barnett hit the ceiling. After a few unprintable epithets, he went away muttering to himself, vowing to get Cal, the sales manager, into the office and blast him.

When they came together at 3:00 that afternoon, Joe started on Cal right away: "What right have you to take one of our biggest customers and refuse to sell to them. I can't believe that a man whose whole business career depends on how much he sells can literally block a sale to one of the largest customers we have. In addition to that, the stuff sat in the warehouse for a whole week and, at today's interest rates, any inventory we've got sitting around that long is, sooner or later, going to break the company.

"I most certainly thought you had more brains than that."

A very upset Cal responded: "Joe, you hired me to sell, not give the God damn stuff away. I don't know whether you know it or not, but Amalgamated filed for bankruptcy last week. I wasn't about to send them a big shipment of our products for which we would never be paid. Now, it may be sitting there in the warehouse, drawing down interest on money, but that sure as hell is a lot cheaper than throwing it away."

Notice, in the example, that there were a dozen ways that Joe could have approached that conversation without leaving himself wide open, and without creating a situation in which both men were upset and one of them embarrassed.

The sixty-second opener is designed to prevent just such situations when they are avoidable. There is no need to start fights when you can preserve friendships, and no need to lose the cooperation of employees, which every company needs in today's atmosphere of competition.

What does the sixty-second opener do for us?

First, it lets the other person know we have spent time preparing for this communication.

Second, it reveals that his or her feelings are important to us and that we are considering them thoughtfully.

Third, because we have planned our objectives and gotten our facts, the other person knows we want an open give-and-take communication.

Fourth, the other person knows we think his or her needs are important because we have explained what's in it for him or her.

The sixty-second opener can rarely be created without preparation. If we know we must cover the elements of O.P.E.N. Communication in sixty seconds, we need thorough preparation.

Mark Twain was once asked to give a talk. "How long a talk?" asked Twain. "Only twenty minutes," was the answer. "Don't have time," said Twain. "Two hours I can do now. Twenty minutes will take me two weeks to prepare."

Preparation for a sixty-second opener does not necessarily take two weeks. Often, it can be done well in a few minutes when you are familiar with the facts of the situation. And that brings us to step #3.

Following the sixty-second opener, the next step in the interaction is a thorough examination of the facts of the situation, to allow both individuals to come to the conclusion, "I will in fact gain value from a commitment to action." Chapter 7 provides an in-depth analysis of this third phase of O.P.E.N. Communication.

Now let's look at some misconceptions about the concept and structure of O.P.E.N. Communication.

The response of more than 8,000 people in seminars over the last seven years reveal one common misconception.

The conference leader poses this question: What image comes to your mind when you hear the words, "open communication"?

Answers include the following:

a. Tell it like it is.

b. An unstructured approach.

c. A feeling of freedom.

d. Total disclosure of all the facts.

e. Free and easy.

f. An honest interaction.

By now, you realize that some of these images are right on, while others are not. O.P.E.N. Communication *is* a highly *structured* approach to interaction between people. In fact, it is the structure that provides for honest interaction ... the feeling of freedom to express one's thoughts, ideas and feelings...the development of positive relationships.

Remember, we know the meanings of words are in minds, not in dictionaries. The key word causing confusion in this case is *structured*.

For instance, suppose you heard this statement: "Everything she says is structured." What would it mean to you? You might think, "She is a conniver—someone who's out to do me in. Someone who's planning to go home with the marbles. Someone who gets up early to beat me at my own game."

But there are many other connotations, and, as we said, connotation is in the mind, not in the dictionary. To others, "structured" might mean "well-organized," "well thought out," "worth listening to." As we said in Chapter 1, words are not very dependable media for communication. They mean different things to different people. In the case of O.P.E.N. Communication, let's see what the word *structured* really means.

The *structure* of O.P.E.N. Communication is a framework, a skeleton, which allows the individual to reach far beyond his or her limited personal capacity. It allows for the transfer of energy most efficiently and effectively ... for the transfer of mass, as in the structure of a bridge.

By creating a structure in this sense, you now have the capacity to extend the resources of each individual. It is, therefore, not a block or interference; it is the very means by which we can most efficiently use energies and efforts to accomplish more.

There is another and seemingly dichotomous misconception existing in the minds of people when they hear the words *O.P.E.N. Communication*. This is the idea that is an off-the-cuff, fly-by-the-seat-of-your-pants, extemporaneous approach.

Again, nothing could be further from the truth. In order to insure that the philosophy of win/win will exist, one must prepare the structure of O.P.E.N. Communication. Without the preparation, what usually happens is misunderstanding.

Once people understand the structure of O.P.E.N. Communication, a fear can develop ... fear of the sixty-second opening. What happens if you use the sixty-second opener with an individual who is a practiced, closed communicator ... one who really believes that every interaction is a win/lose interaction? Won't you really lose control?

The answer is definitely, "NO!" Chapter 8 provides numerous examples to show that a disciplined O.P.E.N. communicator doesn't lose in the interface with a closed communicator. One reason is that the O.P.E.N. communicator sets the stage, or the ground rules, under which both play the game. In fact, as explained in Chapter 8, there are eight reasons why a practiced, open communicator is not manipulated by a practiced, closed communicator.

When should O.P.E.N. Communication be used? It's important to remember that it is not a cure-all or a panacea for all ills. It is a specific discipline designed to accomplish a specific task ... the task of enabling two individuals to interact and reach decisions which will continue to provide value to both.

There are two other types of interaction where this is not the intent.

The first is called WAR! The purpose of war is not to attempt to live with others in the future, but either to destroy them or to control them completely. The attitudes of war not only exist between nations, but can also be the condition for interactions between people.

There is another kind of interaction between people—a CONTEST. In a contest, the rules of the game are very clearly spelled out, and must be adhered to by each player. The obvious objective of the contest is for one player or one side to win. But it's important to remember that in winning a contest, one player does not destroy the other.

Business competition in the free world is an example of contest. There are rules established, both by the business community and the courts, which define the actions each side may take to win. Again, the winner does not destroy the other player's right or capacity to perform. In fact, the natural laws of business demonstrate the difference between contest and war.

O.P.E.N. Communication Is Neither War nor a Contest

IT IS ... a purposeful and powerful approach to the process of communication which results in a win/win situation.

Without the structured procedure of an O.P.E.N. communicator, the chances are you will be perceived as a win/lose person. The final result of this is personal warfare. But you do have a choice. The rest of this book should allow you to understand and practice O.P.E.N. Communication ... and *achieve*.

3
WHY IT WORKS

O.P.E.N. Communication works because it is based upon sound principles in two critical areas: The process of communication, and the dynamics of interpersonal relationships.

The Process of Communication

Communication is the vehicle by which people interact. How does it work?

First, we must understand the purpose of communication. You have communicated when you have been understood. No understanding—no communication.

Remember the old story. Two psychiatrists pass on the street. One says, "Good morning, Sir." The other asks himself, "What did he mean by that?"

Good communication exists when an idea in the mind of one person is transferred to the mind of another person, and the perception of the *meaning* of that idea is the same in the mind of the receiver as it is in the mind of the sender.

We have seen examples of situations where good communication did not occur, because the receiver had an idea in mind that had no relation to the idea in the mind of the communicator.

What happens when good communication *does* occur?

1. Person A conceives of a thought or idea.

2. Person A then forms the idea into a message, using words and/or pictures and/or actions for transmission.

3. Person A then delivers that message, using his chosen media—words, pictures, actions.

4. The receiver, Person B, using the senses of sight, hearing, and maybe touch, receives the message.

5. The message then passes through the experience filters of Person B, where it is tested, evaluated, and organized into a thought or idea, colored by his or her understanding of what that thought or idea really means.

6. To insure that the communication has been effective, Person B then initiates the feedback process, returning the message as he or she understands it back to Person A.

7. The initial sender, Person A, receives it.

8. The initial sender, Person A, then filters that returned message through his or her experiences; and if the final idea and its meaning is the same as that initially sent, effective communication has occurred.

Here's an example:

Mother is sitting in the living room, one evening, reading the paper. She turns the page and sees a picture of a young man. This triggers a thought process which says, "We should telephone our son who is in a distant city and let him know we think about him and find out how he's doing."

The mother then forms the idea into a message and delivers it to her husband, who is sitting across the room.

COMMUNICATION PROCESSES

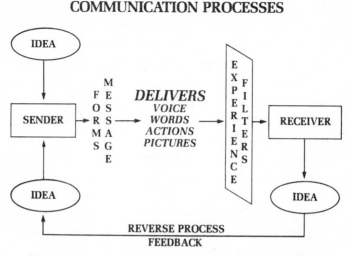

If the ideas are the same, then communication has taken place.

The husband hears the words and the inflection, and filters them through his experiences. He forms the message which be believes he has received into words and delivers it back to his wife, "Then I take it you would like to call John right now."

The wife receives the message through her sense of hearing and filters it through her experiences, confirming receipt of the idea by saying, "Yes, I think that would be a lovely idea." Communication has occurred.

Simple enough... but let's see where even this simple communication could break down.

At Step #1 of the forming of the idea in the mind of the wife, when she looks at the picture of the boy in the newspaper, she thinks, "We haven't heard from John for a long time." This is simply a statement of fact. She now forms it into a communicable idea which she delivers in a plaintive voice, "We haven't heard from John for a long time."

Her husband hears the words and sees the sad look on his wife's face and filters the words, the inflection and the expression through his experiences, which then is registered in his mind as, "She is still trying to mother her son, even though he is 24 years old and has been gone from home for two years."

The husband then forms his thoughts into a message and feeds back, with a rather stern voice, "Now, dear, we have got to let John make it on his own."

The wife now receives these words, and the intonation, and filters them through her experiences; the idea is now recorded as, "He doesn't really care about my feelings and has really put John out of his mind." Her response back, then, is, "I wish you worried about John as much as you do about that damn business of yours."

In this example, we can see how easily good communication can break down:

- When an idea is not clearly formed in the sender's mind.
- When the sender uses inappropriate or confusing words to form the message.
- When the message is delivered with words, gestures or use of the vocal cords which confuse or paint a misleading picture.
- When the receiver places too much emphasis on the way the words were spoken and the gestures that accompany them, rather than listening to the words themselves.
- When the filtering process of the receiver's experiences causes him or her to perceive a totally different message or feeling behind the message.

The problem is that the communication process hasn't stopped with the initial misreading of the message. The receiver will respond ... even if it's just with a gesture, a shrug of the shoulders, a sigh, or with heated words, as in the example above. And the result can be mutual misunderstanding and hard feelings.

One additional critical element is identified when we diagram the communication process. The most important things that people communicate are *ideas* and their feelings about those ideas. Facts are merely the building blocks for creating ideas.

Ideas always include relationships of things or people, past, present or future. Whenever we communicate an idea, we feel either positive or negative about that idea.

The reason we insist that what we communicate is ideas rather than facts goes back to the dictionary definition of communication—"the process by which *meanings* are exchanged between people." This means that the process of communication we have just diagrammed should insure that both the sender and the receiver understand not only the idea but also the feeling behind that idea—the *meaning* of the message.

And this means that when we *listen*, we should listen for the meanings and feelings that the other person is communicating, as well as the facts.

Unfortunately, the older we get, the more we tend to rely on our own experiences to judge the communication, and to listen to our own feelings rather than considering the sender's. We are like the small boy whose father said to the waiter, "Wrap up the rest of the steak for the dog." "Oh, goody!" said the boy, "We're going to get a dog."

Now let's review how the O.P.E.N. Communication structure insures that the *process of communication* occurs, and how it builds in checks to insure that blocks to understanding are identified and overcome.

Remember, the first step in O.P.E.N. is *preparation* for the interaction with the other person. You clearly think your way through the specific action you want the other person to take. That's the "O" or objective.

The "E" in O.P.E.N. —*expect*— forces the sender to think about the experience filters of the receiver that will act on the message that is broadcast. This assists the sender in forming the message in such a way that the experience filters will be identified and recognized, and not block the understanding process.

The "N" in O.P.E.N.—*need*—again forces the sender to put himself or herself in the shoes of the receiver to be able to answer the question, "What's in it for the other person?" —to make sure that the action is consistent with the receiver's self-image, goals and desires.

The "P" in O.P.E.N. —*plan*— causes us to form the message, taking into consideration the results of our preparation in terms of expectancy, need and objective, and including proof that the needs of the other person are being met.

The 60-second opener can then unlock the doors to understanding. It can prove by our *actions* that our intent is understanding and that we want to make sure that both parties receive value.

The execution of the plan requires constant feedback about ideas and the feelings behind those ideas. This is a continual check. If for some reason communication isn't working, we can identify the breakdown, because we know where and how the process can break down.

Both people can feel secure in the interaction, because the structure itself is the *control mechanism*.

The Dynamics of Interpersonal Relationships

The second reason the structure of O.P.E.N. Communication works is that it is completely consistent with, and uses, the principles of the dynamics of interaction between people, the first and most critical of which is the principle of self-preservation/fulfillment. This principle states that

THE THREE SIDED PERSONALITY

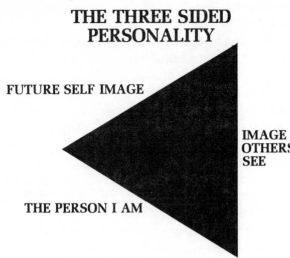

FUTURE SELF IMAGE

IMAGE OTHERS SEE

THE PERSON I AM

most individuals (unless the mind is diseased) want to feel good about themselves.

In order to understand fully the law of self-preservation/fulfillment, let's see how people perceive themselves ... the process we call self-understanding. There are two major elements to understanding oneself:

- The three-sided personality
- Human needs

The best way the three-sided personality can be explained is with a little poem.

"Down the road went three men,

Down the road went he

The man he was,

The man they saw,

The man he wanted to be."

Each individual has three sides to his or her personality, not just one. Each one of those sides interacts with the others to create a three-dimensional or whole personality.

One side of personality is the *image that we have of ourselves living in the future.*

We state this image with our goals and objectives ... goals and objectives in terms of:

1. What we want *to have* ... the physical things in life.

2. What we want *to be* in relationship to *ourselves.*

3. What we want *to be* in relationship to *others* ("position relationships").

4. What we want to be *doing* with the skills and capacities that we have developed to this point in our life.

1. The "to have" goals and objectives. These objectives are usually purchased with dollars, although not always. For example, I want to have a house in the country, a membership in the country club, a yacht, enough money to retire when I am 55 years old. These objectives are critical to us, because in a sense they become our score card to determine what we have been doing with our life. They also can provide a certain element of security, because the physical world in which we live has a tremendous amount to do with our internal feeling of security.

2. The goals and objectives of our relationship to ourselves. I want to be happy. I want to feel fulfilled. I want to understand that I have value and to feel that I have not wasted my life and energy ... to feel that I have accomplished those things that are important to me, regardless of what I might have or what other people might think.

3. The goals and objectives of our relationships to other people. I want to be Vice-President of Sales. I want to be the most professional System Design Engineer in the company. I want to be a good mother or a good father. These "to be's" are given to us by other people. The "to be an officer in a company" will be given to you by the Board

of Directors of that company and the employees of that company. The "to be a good mother or father" will be given to you by your children.

4. The "to do" goals and objectives. This fourth category of goals and objectives is the most critical. These are the statements of what we want to be doing in the future with the skills and talents which we have developed. For example, "I want to use my knowledge of the effects of claim ratios and costs so that the company can make positive decisions, both for itself and for the insured."

"I want to combine my understanding of the electronics industry with my capacity to train and educate others to help people develop their skills in this demanding electronics field."

"I want to use my highly developed analytical skills in performing research work on the effects of amino acids."

In each of the above examples, we see that the individual has an understanding of the specific skills and talents which he or she has developed. The individuals want to put themselves in a position where they can use those skills and capacities to a greater and greater degree.

The reason the "to do's" are so important is that it is what we will *be doing* in the future that will earn us the dollars to get the "to have's." It is what we will be doing in the future that will earn us the respect and trust from others that we need to get the position objectives in terms of what we want *to be* ... it is what you *do* with your children that earns you the respect and trust to be "a good father."

Most importantly, it is what we will be doing in the future that will enable us to achieve our *personal* "to be" objectives...to be happy, to be fulfilled, to feel that we have value.

Now the relationship of those objectives in each individual becomes very critical to us. A number of years ago, the Chicago Tribune ran a series of articles, the initial intent of which was to interview men in all walks of life to determine what were the happiest years of a man's life. As a result of this interviewing procedure, they found out what most behavioral scientists' studies of the last few years have shown. They identified the unhappiest year of a man's life. This unhappy period lasted somewhere between six months and a year, and it occurred between age 35 and age 45 for 85 to 90 percent of the men interviewed.

The reason this was an unhappy and traumatic period in a man's life was that it was during this period that he realized that he had not attained his goals and objectives... not the goals and objectives of what he wanted to have, but the goals and objectives of what he wanted to be doing. The individual had established an image of himself living in the future back when he was 18, 20, 22 years old. Suddenly at age 40 or thereabouts, the individual stopped and said, "What am I *doing* here!"

Note the emphasis on the word *doing*. It made no difference how much money the individual was making or what position within the corporation or organization the individual had. It was a feeling of, "Oh, my God, I am wasting my life! I'm boxed into a position that is not allowing me to do those things which really give me satisfaction and happiness."

The decade between 35 and 45 is the time when many individuals make a major career change. The reason is that they are unsatisfied with what they are doing in their present positions. There are thousands of examples of individuals who reach an executive position in an organization, making an income in the six figure bracket, who then totally change their life style.

Why?

To do what they want to do.

The person who was Vice President of Research and Development for a major high technology company, who at age 40 quit his six figure job, bought a farm in Maine, and started teaching high school mathematics

... the Dean of Administration in a Midwestern University, who left that job to go back to being a full-time professor...the Sales Manager who went back to being a full-time salesman. All give the same reason. "I was really not *happy* performing those administrative and managerial functions. I really enjoy doing what I am good at doing ... and that's what I'm doing now."

There are many reasons why individuals have difficulty establishing the "to do's" goals and objectives for their lives. Two critical ones to look at are:

1. At a given point in our lives, we don't really understand what skills and talents we have.

2. We establish our goals and objectives in terms of what we want *to be*, based upon other people's desires and expectations of us.

Let's look at the first condition ... lack of understanding of the skills and capacities we have.

One of the responsibilities I had when I was an officer in a major corporation was college recruiting. At the initial stages of interviewing seniors, I would ask, "What do you want to be doing five years from now?" The typical response was, "I want to be Vice-President of Sales!" or "I want your job!" When I asked, "Why do you want to be Vice-President of Sales?," the typical answer was, "Because I want to make a lot of money!" or "Because of the prestige!" When the senior was then asked to explain what a Vice-President of Sales *does*, there was no answer or, at best, a very vague idea.

I soon learned that this was an unfair question to ask. A college senior has not had enough experience with the business world to enable him or her to develop a sound understanding of what skills he or she has and needs to be successful. People cannot effectively determine what they want to be doing in the future if they really do not have a very clear understanding of what skills and capacities they have today.

Our goals and objectives will constantly evolve and change as we live each day and learn more and more about our skills and capacities. Success breeds success. We have a tendency to continue to do those things which give us success.

Bill Alexander, a minister in Oklahoma City, gave one of the best definitions of happiness that we've heard:

> "It is that state of imbalance where I achieved my objective of yesterday, and in achieving that objective, I have established my objective for what I want to be *doing* tomorrow."

The second major reason why people have difficulty establishing their "to do" goals is over-emphasis on the "to be" and "to have" goals. Much of the time, these goals are determined by or are forced upon us by other people. Mothers and fathers say that we have to *be somebody*. Society gives great acclaim to those individuals who have achieved high positions. The position, therefore, becomes the goal for the individual, rather than the individual choosing a position that will allow him or her to use and enjoy the skills and talents which he or she has.

In an interview, Ted Hesburgh, Chancellor of Notre Dame University, admitted that he had established the goal for his life back when he was in high school. His objective was to be Chancellor of Notre Dame University. At age 37, he had achieved his objective.

Here is the most important insight from Ted Hesburgh. He did not establish the objective of being Chancellor of Notre Dame for the sheer joy of having that position. He established it because he believed that in that position he could *use his skills and talents as an educator* better than in any other position that he could imagine. Ted Hesburgh is happy because he has a position that allows him to perform as a professional educator.

There we have the first side of the three-sided personality—our image of ourselves living in the future. In practicing the discipline of O.P.E.N. Communication, it is important for us to understand as much about the other individual's image of himself or herself living in the future as we possibly can. One of his or her needs is to achieve those goals.

Now let's look at the second side of the three-sided triangle—*my understanding of the person that I am today.*

Each one of us is a result of all the experiences that he or she has lived through. Dr. Mark Silber of Mark Silber and Associates of Des Plaines, Illinois, has provided a framework to help us understand the impact of our experiences on our self-understanding.

His framework is the concept that each one of us has *three* experience tapes in our minds. These tapes are much like the tape drives on a computer. The important thing is that they are separate tapes, with different experiences stored on each.

The first tape is our *mental tape.* This tape controls our *thought processes.* On this tape are stored the experiences we've had which have developed our knowledge base. Humans think in terms of words, symbols and spatial relationships (pictures/diagrams). When an individual has something stored on his or her mental tape, we say he or she has knowledge. The way that we know someone has knowledge is whether he or she can indicate what is stored in that tape with words, pictures, symbols or spatial relationships.

For example, if an individual says he or she knows how to do a "return on an invested capital analysis," he or she should be able to use the symbols—do the math—or there is nothing stored on the mental tape. Our mental tape controls what we think about, what we know ... and we think with words, pictures and relatives.

The second experience tape is the *skill/behavior tape.* On this tape is stored what we are capable of doing.

This tape controls our *actions and behaviors.*

Let's look at any sport to see the difference between the mental tape and the skill tape. An individual can read books on a sport and gain enough knowledge to explain exactly how to play that sport...how to hit a drive in golf or swing a backhand in tennis. We now say the person has a mental understanding of that sport. However, that mental understanding does not do much good in an actual game unless the skill tape also comes into play. When an individual goes from a mental understanding of the sport to an actual capacity to participate in the sport, we say the muscles have learned what the mind knows. The experience tape now has developed the expertise actually to *do* the activity.

The only way we can determine whether an individual has developed anything on his or her skill tape is to watch the actions or the behavior of the individual. Words only confirm that something is stored on the mental tape. Most of us have had lots of experience in our lives with individuals who have been able to tell us how to do something—for instance, the mechanics of how to be an effective listener—yet, who, in actual operation with others, demonstrate that their behavior has not yet learned what the individuals knew in their minds (for example, they are very poor listeners).

Each one of these first two tapes is a separate tape. Therefore, an individual can have something stored on his or her skill or behavior tape and not be able to explain in words (the task of the mental tape) what he or she is doing.

The obvious example of this is the natural athlete, who intuitively has developed the skills but has great difficulty explaining to someone else exactly what he or she is doing in order to be the top in the profession.

Another example (which might hit much closer to home for many of us) is the manager who has learned intuitively the six steps in the planning process, but when asked to explain what he or she is doing, has great difficulty explaining exactly what was done. Yet a detailed analysis of the person's actions proves that he or she is executing the six-step process of planning.

The third tape is our *value tape*. On this tape are stored the experiences we've had which now control our *involvement*. These experiences determine what we believe and what we value, and this in turn determines where we will spend our energy in order to become involved in a particular situation; where we will not become involved due to our judgments of morality and ethics; where we will take risks and where we will not take risks; where we will expend our energy and where we will not expend our energy.

> Let's look at the young man who is on the track team in high school and is a natural athlete. His father, who was not a natural athlete but was also on the track team when he was a young man, says to the young man, "Son, why don't you practice and put the energy into the 400 meter event? You have the skill ... if you just wanted to be, you could be Number One in the entire *state*."

> The son's reply to his father is, "Pop, I couldn't care less about being Number One in that event. If I had to spend the time, energy and effort to be Number One in the 400 meter, there are a lot of other things that I couldn't do that I really enjoy. Who says I have to be Number One? As long as I am good enough to make the team, that's what's important to me. And then I can do a lot of other things, too. Why should I spend all of my energy on one or two things?"

Here we have an example of different value systems at play. The father's value tape says, "In whatever you start to become involved, spend the energy and the time to try to become Number One. Now, don't be wiped out if you don't achieve the Number One position, but you have to try. You don't go in saying, 'I'm going to be average or Number Ten.'"

The son's value tape says something totally different. His tape says that the important thing in life is participating in lots of activities, so that you can expand your horizons and taste many of the things of life. Both the father's and the son's tapes were developed as a result of the experiences they had in their lives.

In O.P.E.N. Communication, people will take actions that are consistent with their values, actions that use those skills and knowledge. Knowing what's stored on those tapes is critical in determining a person's needs.

The key point is that each side of the three-sided triangle affects the other sides. Thus, as we gain additional experiences and these experiences are stored on our experience tapes, they also affect the first side of the triangle —the goals and objectives we have for our lives. The more that we understand of what's stored on our three tapes — mental, skill and value—the greater impact that will have on the goals and objectives we establish for ourselves in terms of what we want to have, what we want to be, and what we want to be doing.

What we are asking another individual to do, therefore, should be consistent with and help that individual to build upon his or her concept of his or her knowledge, skill and values, as well as help to achieve his or her goals.

The third side of the three-sided personality is *our understanding of how other people see us*. Notice that this is not our projection of what we *want* other people to see. This, in fact, is our understanding of how other people *do* perceive us.

If we are going to live in the world of other people, it is critical to know what they think about us, because this will affect what they do in relationship to us. If we don't know this, we're shooting in the dark when we attempt to relate to other people and get them to take actions which will satisfy our needs.

The only way that we can get an understanding of how other people perceive us is to have them tell us. We call this feedback ... honest feedback about how the other person perceives us and how what we are doing affects him or her.

There are many blocks to this feedback process, and they make it difficult for us to have a real understanding of the third side of our personality. The single largest block to the feedback process is fear or insecurity. If we are fearful or insecure, we must take actions to protect ourselves. This protective stance blocks feedback from both directions. It blocks the other individual from telling us honestly how he or she perceives us. It also blocks our capacity to receive the broadcast coming from the other individual, because we put up defense filters. These defense filters then cause us to see and hear only those things which we perceive are correct.

The process of O.P.E.N. Communication provides a structure for interaction which eliminates fear and insecurity. Thus, it allows us to interact openly and objectively so that we can, in fact, see and understand this third side of our personality.

The concept of the three-sided personality, therefore, indicates that there are three ways that we understand ourselves. The first is an understanding of the image that we have of ourselves living in the future. Because we are creatures with free will, we can take actions that will have an impact on our future. The second is the understanding that we are the result of all the experiences we've lived through. Therefore, we must understand what those experiences have caused us to become in terms of our knowledge, our skills and our values. The third side is our reality check, because we do live in the world of others, and we must see ourselves through the eyes of others.

The process of establishing a relationship, the climate by which other individuals will be willing to tell us exactly how they perceive us, is a very demanding process. To assist in understanding this process, we must look at the second element of self-understanding which is called *human needs*.

Human Needs

A psychologist of the early twentieth century, Watson, classified human needs into four main categories. It is important to note that when we say human needs, we are assuming that the biological needs of food, water and shelter are being met. Human needs, by definition, only means those needs that exist when we decide we want to live in the world of other people. A hermit, for example, does not have any human needs. Once we've made the decision to live in the world of other people, what other people do affects us and what we do affects them. (The entire chapter on expectations deals with the dynamics of this interaction.)

Our willingness and capacity to deal with other people depends upon the human need drive within each one of us. Watson identified the elements of human needs as:

> Security
> Acceptance
> Recognition
> Growth/new experience

Let's look at each one of the four elements to determine exactly what is meant by the key words, and most importantly, to see how they interrelate and affect each other. If these are the total of the human need drives, these four can only add up to one hundred percent. They cannot add up to more than one hundred percent or less than one hundred percent of the need drive within the individual, whatever the magnitude of that need drive is.

Security is the first human need. This word means different things to different people. Watson describes security as "my feeling that I am in control of my environment." You will notice that it makes no difference whether you are in control of your environment or not. As long as you feel that you are in control of your environment, by definition you are secure. You do not have the need for security. For example, when you are on a 747 at 39,000 feet, we might question whether you are really in control of that environment. But, as long as you feel, "I, by my free will, made the decision to be here, thus I am in control of my environment," you are secure. The individual who has a fear of flying, has this fear because he believes that if he is 39,000 feet in the air, he has lost control. Therefore, he is insecure and will not put himself in that environment.

Let something happen either to me or to my environment, so that I feel that I am losing control, and I now have the need for security. I am insecure and must take whatever action is necessary to get me back to feeling that I am in control.

When we are insecure, we will take whatever action is necessary to bring us back to a position of security. Those actions can either be *positive actions* which build upon our capacity to control our environment continuously or they can be *defensive actions* which we take to protect ourselves.

Most of the time the actions are defensive ... protective. Defensive actions do not build our capacity to control the future. Others recognize that we are becoming defensive. This recognition then either causes them to continue the attack in order to control us (the technique of the closed or manipulative individual or philosophy) or causes them to believe that something is wrong. They then react with suspicion, lack of trust or lack of respect.

Acceptance is the second human need. Acceptance says that what I am is important to other people ... me, my values, my beliefs, my foibles. I, as an individual, am accepted by others. The epitome of acceptance is love. Because love is unconditional acceptance, there are no strings attached to it. Again, all of us to one degree or another have the need to be accepted by other people.

Recognition is the third human need. What I *do* is recognized by others as having value. My performance, my accomplishments, are seen by other people as adding value to themselves or adding value to the situation in which they are involved. Again, once we've made the decision to live in the world of other people, other people's concepts and understanding about what we do is critical to us. Therefore, we have the need to be recognized by others for what we do and accomplish.

The fourth need is the need to **experience the new**...to grow. This means that as living organisms we must constantly put ourselves into new experiences. We then gain the exhilaration of those new experiences and constantly expand our horizons. We increase our capacity to understand and deal with the world.

The need to *experience the new* is diametrically opposed to the need for *security.* Thus, if what you are doing to a person makes him or her feel insecure, don't be surprised if he or she becomes defensive, and doesn't do what you want done.

Now, the balance among these four separate elements of the need drive (remember, they can only add up to one hundred percent) is determined to a considerable degree by the environment in which we live—other people. Let's take the young child at age one through age five. The balance of the need drive of that child puts about ninety percent of it behind new experience. The child is like a sponge, constantly reaching out.

There is little need to be *accepted,* because the child really has not developed a personality at this point to worry about acceptance. Of course, there is an exception to this. The child must feel loved. Take away love and the child may die.

The need for *recognition,* again, is at a very low level, because the child has not developed any skills that he or she needs to have recognized. As long as he or she is loved and his or her physical needs are met, the need for *security* is also at a very low level.

What happens the day the child goes to school? Now he or she is in a very structured environment which demands that the child learn, and gain recognition for this learning. The structured environment also demands that the child's actions be such that they will be accepted by the institution and the teachers. This structured environment now also demands, to a much greater degree, that the child gain the acceptance of his or her peers within the structured environment. The result is that the child's feeling of security usually goes to hell in a hand-basket.

Let's look at the same child eight years later, when he or she is a senior in grade school. As a result of the child's experiences, he or she has now learned to deal with that environment and is secure. The child has developed acceptance and recognition, and is willing to try new experiences. But, lo and behold, he or she graduates and becomes a freshman in high school... a totally new and demanding experience. Security becomes critical and the need to gain acceptance and recognition is paramount once more.

In summary, we see that the balance among the four need drives — security, recognition, acceptance and new experience—depends upon two major conditions:

1. My understanding of myself and my ability to control the environment. The more I understand my skills and abilities, the more I understand my goals and objectives, the more secure and confident I will be in my capacity to interact effectively with other people.

2. My perception of what is happening in the environment around me. If I perceive that my environment is changing and becoming hostile, that I am being placed in a win/lose position, *that could* affect my first human need, the need for security. I will then try to protect myself rather than try to develop new relationships.

O.P.E.N. Communication builds on the concept of human needs and enables you to create an environment which supports the security of the other person (he or she knows where you are coming from because you've stated your objectives). Your listener knows what is going to be happening during the interaction, because you've stated the roles each of you will play. He or she knows the plan under which both of you will be operating. You've met the other person's needs for recognition and acceptance by addressing yourself to his or her personal and job-oriented needs.

When you have accomplished this, you are satisfying the needs for security, acceptance and recognition. Now the individual can use his or her drive for new experience to decide openly on the actions which he or she will take in the future...actions which will, in fact, result in a win/win situation.

The key to putting it all together is an understanding of strengths and weaknesses. The more we understand our capacities, the more willing we'll be to put ourselves into new situations, because we are secure in our capacity to control the new experiences.

Now, with every interaction we undertake, we can determine our specific actions and what we want other people to do in order to help us to achieve our goals and objectives.

The O.P.E.N. Communication process builds self-understanding in ourselves and others. It forces us to clarify our needs, and to determine what specific actions other people can take to enable us to achieve those needs. It forces us to have the same concern for the other individual, recognizing that his or her needs are paramount and that he or she will only take actions consistent with his or her goals and objectives, actions which give him or her recognition and acceptance, and provide for new experiences.

Recognizing that past experiences can cause us to have "mind-sets" or blocks, we think more clearly. We recognize our own skills and abilities and those of our listener.

The result is a continuing development of self-awareness and maturity based upon self-understanding. This increases our objectivity and our own self-control.

Why the O.P.E.N. Structure Produces a Win/Win Situation

The comment most often heard after individuals have been exposed to the concept of O.P.E.N. Communication is: "It works. It really works!"

Well, then, why does it work?

It should not be difficult to understand that in any situation where both sides win, the results are going to be successful.

But this success presupposes two conditions ... first, that we define exactly what we mean by a win/win philosophy, and secondly, that we prove that a win/win philosophy is a reality, and not just a pipe dream.

Let's address the first issue — what is meant by win/win. Most people initially have problems with this concept because they think of it in terms of a contest. Obviously, in a contest, there is a winner and a loser. Remember, we said that there were three reasons why people interact with each other (war, contest and when they want to live together in the future).

When we are going to live with the other person in the future, we are dealing with different ground rules than when the interaction is a contest. So, let's see what those ground rules are and if, in fact, they can result in win/win situations.

A person wins when *his or her needs will be met by the actions he or she is taking right now* ... when the investment in time, energy and effort will provide an adequate return for that investment.

In other words, the individual must receive value in the future, as a result of the action that he or she is taking today.

Let's look at a few examples, then we can analyze those examples to determine:

- Are they win/win situations?

- Why can we call them win/win situations?

Here's the first example.

In a selling situation, the buyer agrees to allow the salesperson to make a major presentation to the vice presidents of Finance and Operations within his company. What the buyer is giving up in this instance is the control of the situation. He is allowing the salesperson to have direct contact with his two major superiors. The buyer will only make that decision when he believes the result of the salesperson's contact with those two officers will be a positive reflection on his own decision making and judgment.

Now, if the salesperson's interaction with the two vice presidents is a positive one, then, in fact, both salesperson and buyer have won. The buyer has received greater value as a result of the decision he has made, and the salesperson has also received greater value because he has now had the opportunity to get to the decision makers in the corporation with his company's proposal. This is a win/win situation.

Here's another example.

A father asks his son to wash the family car. If the son does what the father has requested, he is spending time, energy and effort to accomplish the task. This is time that he could have used doing something else. If the son does wash the family car, his winning might be the father's agreement to have him use that family car at some time in the future.

Of course, if the father is not willing and does not reciprocate in the future by allowing the son ever to use the family car, then at some point, the son is going to say, "This is not a win/win situation, because I am not receiving anything of value in return."

Here's another example of a win/win situation in labor union negotiating.

Management agrees to establish a review board for employee grievances, consisting of two members of the union and two members of management and one independent arbitrator agreeable to both parties. In this instance, management is giving up their prerogative to discipline and/or fire an employee for reasons which they believe are justified; labor is receiving the value of having an equal voice in the protection of the job security of their members. Now, this can only become a win/win situation when in the actual execution of the review committee the rights of both parties, labor and management, are respected and acted upon in the judicial fashion.

In all three examples, we saw a win/win situation in which both parties received something of greater value than what they gave up in making the decision to take the specific action.

The definition of win/win, therefore, is *when both parties make a decision to give something for something of greater value.*

A "win" can be either material or emotional. When a boy, in his interaction with another boy, agreeably exchanges a jackknife for a baseball, each feels he has made a material "win." The one who received the baseball wanted the ball more than the jackknife and vice versa—each for his own reasons.

Therefore, the decision as to whether an individual is getting greater value really is based upon two major elements:

Element 1: The *previous* experiences the individual has had which result in his development of the *yardstick* or the criteria for evaluation of what is of value to him or her and what is not.

Element 2: The image that the individual has of himself or herself *living in the future.* This determines what types of things will be important to that individual in order to match that image ... what will help him or her to achieve those goals and objectives.

Let's look at a few examples of how these two major elements affect each individual's concept of value. The first example is from the real estate industry.

Tom Lutz and his family have lived for ten years of their married life in a small Midwestern town. In the course of these ten years, they have owned two different houses. The second house (the one they are living in now) has 3,000 square feet, on two acres of ground, with eight rooms and a two-car attached garage. They paid $80,000 for this home two years ago and now, in this Midwestern town, the house is worth $90,000.

Tom's company has asked him to transfer, to accept a promotion to Regional Manager for the Los Angeles area.

The family now has a *need* to find a place to live in the Los Angeles area. When they look to see what is of value in terms of real estate, the condition they find is this: A 3,000 square foot home, with eight rooms and an attached garage on a half acre of ground, costs $240,000.

The decision only made by past experience would be that this is not of value. We should not make the decision to give $240,000 for that piece of property.

Here now, is where the second element of value comes into being ... what our goals, needs and objectives are in the future.

Now, the criteria for the decision revolve around the choices that the family has as to where they can live. When we say live, this means much more than just having a place to sleep and eat. It is having a home that matches the needs of the four members of that family—father, mother, son and daughter; the needs of living in a community where the educational needs of the family can be met, living in a community where the sociological needs of the family can be met.

So now, we see that the decision making is not based

upon previous experience. It must be based upon the answers to the various needs that the family has when making a decision about where they are *going to live*. The criteria for decision making are based upon the image that the family has of themselves living in the future.

Now, if the family does make the decision to buy a particular home and if, when they start living in that home, they find that it fulfills the promises that were made, they say, "Yes, we have received greater value than the $240,000 which we gave up."

The most important point to be made is that *value* occurs when I live with this decision in the future. If it meets my needs, it is of *value*.

In the decision making process it is critical that both individuals have the opportunity to examine and make decisions on the priorities of their needs both today and in the future. Here again, the structure of O.P.E.N. Communication not only allows this to happen but forces it to happen in the execution of the plan for open communication.

The reason for this is that the needs of the listener are constantly addressed and identified so that the listener can at the conclusion make the decision, "Yes, this is going to be a win/win situation...I'm going to receive greater value in the future than what I am giving up today."

The last consideration in the process of O.P.E.N. Communication is free will. By executing the O.P.E.N. system in all three phases, both individuals in the interaction have the *free will* to make the decisions that they want to make. They take ownership of that decision. This ownership says that I must continuously work to make the decision a win/win decision, not only for myself but for the other individual, for this is consistent with the intent of both of us.

The powerful communicator is the person adept at determining what "win" means to the receiver. There can be times when the communicator cannot determine a "win," and then the interaction probably isn't going to be meaningful.

Think about it. Do you seek interaction with anyone which isn't going to give you a material gain or an emotional stimulus? Why do you join a club? Probably because you hope to be part of a group of people with whom you can identify and from whom you can gain emotionally, or from whose company you can claim some prestige, or in which there are business contracts valuable to you.

It might be said we become more powerful in our community in proportion to the "wins" we can provide others in that community.

We live in a world with other people. They affect us; we affect them. Sooner or later, everything we have in life will depend to a great extent on our interactions with others. We have to be successful if we use those interactions in such a way that both sides "win."

4
OBJECTIVES
The Key to Achievement

"IF YOU DON'T KNOW WHERE YOU'RE GOING, ANY ROAD WILL TAKE YOU THERE." Yogi Berra

How many people just paddle along, keeping alive day after day, doing little to better themselves because... for what should they better themselves? In the absence of objectives, there's no need to develop any capabilities.

When you stop to think about it, there is no word which signifies power more than the word "objectives." People become great because of objectives, or insignificant because of the lack of them. This principle extends itself even to leadership. Can you imagine leadership without objectives? To what or to where would one lead others?

Genghis Khan from his teens wanted to conquer the world, and he almost did it. If Hitler had tempered his objectives with judgment and humanity, he might have conquered the world. He never lost track of what he wanted to do.

The college student of today is often criticized for lacking objectives. If that's true, what is that student doing in school? He or she is just spending a lot of money on an exercise leading nowhere.

Look at a normal day's performance. Two kinds of people arise every morning: the one who knows specifically what he or she wants to accomplish for the day, and the other who rises just to live until dinnertime.

Whatever area of endeavor one chooses to enter, he or she is nothing until the area is defined. Once defined, every effort can be a step in the right direction.

The "O" in O.P. E.N. stands for objective. The theory of objectives holds true even in the simplest, everyday communication. If we don't have a reason or objective for communicating, why bother? One can even say "hello" with an objective. It can be said to create goodwill, to create ill will, to show disdain, to show affection. How one says "hello" connotes one's feelings and, therefore, some objective.

Knowing what our objectives are sounds so simple. Yet research has proven that the great percentages of our interactions do not have clearly defined objectives.

The lack of objectives is the single most damaging error in an attempt to gain understanding and build trust relationships.

"Would you mind coming into my office?"

"Could we spend twenty minutes after lunch to discuss the Ajax project?"

If you were on the receiving end of either one of these two requests, your immediate thoughts are *why* ... what is it that you are going to ask me *to do?*

The reason we respond this way is because we know that most of the interactions we have in life are purposeful.

The two requests given above are examples of interactions in our formal relationships ... the structure of the organizations in which we live. Every time someone in business asks to talk to us we instinctively know that there is a reason. He or she wants us to do something ... give specific information ... commit ourselves to do something ... provide an opinion which commits us to a course of action later on.

That's why the structure of O.P. E.N. Communication starts with O ... the objective.

If I have asked for a conversation with you, I'd better know in advance what I want you *to do*. You will instinctively understand that there is a reason for my asking us to get together. If I can't or don't tell you up front what I want you to do (and I can't do that unless I have prepared), you will:

1. Assume that there is a hidden agenda ... something that I've got to con you into, because it will not particularly help you. You, therefore, will become defensive.

2. Guess at what you think I want. Most of the time the guess will be wrong, and will lead to frustration or conflict. "If you think you understood what I said, you were wrong because I didn't say what I wanted to say."

3. Get the picture loud and clear that I am not prepared. I don't have my act together. Therefore, I am willing to waste your time or, more importantly, put *on you* the *burden* of determining what you can do to help me.

So we see that if we have not established the objective for our interaction with another person, the chances are that the result of the interaction will be negative.

A simple but effective method of defining objectives is to ask yourself:

What am I trying to accomplish ... what do *I* want?

What can *you* do to help me get it?

If the answer to either of these questions is vague, you're running a tremendous risk ... the risk of *assuming* that something positive is going to happen. The chances of this happening are 10 to 1 against you.

If your answer to the question, "What am I trying to accomplish?" is vague, the chances are:

1. You've not done a good job in your own development of self-understanding.

2. You've done a poor job in determining your business strategies, objectives and plans.

Even if we do a good job in determining in advance what our needs are, and have clearly established our own objectives, there still can be many problems with establishing the objective for our listener.

See if you can determine what the objective is for this interaction.

Sam Jones, salesman for the Ajax Company, was put on probation three months ago. The specific goals that he was supposed to achieve during the three month period were spelled out and put in writing. The District Manager, Ed Black, worked with Sam during the three months to attempt to help him to perform in accordance with company criteria.

The three months are up and Sam has not met the criteria that were established. The result of not meeting the criteria, which was termination of employment if the criteria were not met, was understood by Sam Jones.

District Manager Ed Black has asked Sam to come to his office. The action the District Manager wants to take is to communicate to Sam that he is terminated, and to give him the termination package.

Now, what are District Manager Ed Black's objectives for this interaction?

If you decided the objective was to terminate Sam Jones, you were wrong. That is the action step which the District Manager is going to take. Remember, the objective in O.P.E.N. Communication is the specific action you want the *other* person to take.

Therefore, the objective is "to have Sam Jones understand and accept the reasons why he was unsuccessful in this job, in the hope that he will become more capable of putting himself in a position where he can be successful."

There was an actual situation where a manager did not prepare for the interaction utilizing O.P.E.N. He had not established his objective, and the result of the unprepared termination interview was a $4,000,000 class action suit against the company and the manager.

We have now seen an example of the first of many reasons why objective setting can be difficult.

I Assume That the Specific *Action* I Want to Take Is the Objective of Our Interaction.

We see this error in objective setting often with novice salespeople, who will say:

"The objective of my presentation to this customer is to present our new fall promotion." That is not an objective for the interaction. That's a step the salesman is going to take. In order to have an objective, he must spell out specifically what he wants the buyer to do as a result of his presentation of the fall promotion.

Here's another example of assuming that the action I want to take is the objective for my interaction with the other person.

Ed Tate is the Director of Personnel of a large manufacturing company. He has asked to see the Plant Superintendent, Sam Bowman. Ed has found out that Sam has told his Department Managers that they must do an employment check on people that they are considering hiring. To do that employment check, they must telephone the last person that the individual worked for to get his or her opinion of the applicant.

Ed mistook the objective of the session with Sam as "*to tell* Sam that the policy of the company is that no personal reference check be done on any applicant."

Sam's response: "What do you mean I can't check previous work experience. That's the problem with you personnel people...don't do this, don't do that."

The result was a shouting bout that could be heard four blocks away.

Ed's objective should have been "to have Sam *understand* and *agree* to an *approach* to reference checking that would not include personal telephone calls on the applicant's previous employer."

Let's look at some additional assumptions that make setting objectives so difficult.

I Assume That if I Give You the Intent of What I Want You to Do, You Will Know Exactly What to Do.

The story reported to be true about Sony's introduction into the U. S. market many years ago is a beautiful example of providing only intent.

> The main copywriter at the advertising agency which Sony had picked had been given the objective, "design a hard-hitting slogan which would immediately attract the attention of the American people."
>
> After much deliberation, thought, work and effort, the copywriter brought forth the following slogan:
>
> "Brought to you by the same beautiful people who brought you Pearl Harbor."

Obviously, that was not the type of action which the agency or the manufacturer wanted.

Here's another example:

> "My objective is to have you indicate your confidence in my ability to run the political campaign."

This is not an objective, for it does not establish the specific course of action you want the individual to take in evidence of his or her confidence. The other individual could put up a blue smoke screen of lots of general comments which later on he or she could say were honest comments but did not imply any action on his or her part.

Here's how that general statement of intent could become a genuine objective:

"To indicate your confidence in my ability to run the political campaign, by committing yourself to attend the fund-raising banquet."

Now the individual knows that when he or she makes a commitment to attend the fund-raising banquet (a specific action), this indicates his or her confidence in the person's ability to run the campaign.

To avoid the error of assuming that people will know what you want them to do when you provide only the intent of their actions, the objective must be measurable. Here we borrow the definition of an objective from the management sciences: "A statement of a measurable condition which we want in existence at a given point in time."

For example:

"To have you develop and agree to a specific action plan by the end of our session, which you believe you can execute to accomplish the intent."

"To have you make a decision to spend $20,000 on a special promotional program in the next three weeks."

"To have you agree to make no decision until the results of our test market are in."

With each of these examples we have dealt with the need to be able to measure and determine whether the conditions have been achieved or not.

I Assume That if I Tell You the Result That I'm Looking for, You Will Know What to Do to Achieve That Result.

This is another major reason why objective setting is not easy and usually is not accomplished correctly.

The owner of a small manufacturing firm decided to take early retirement and put the firm's future in the hands of John Read, a highly-qualified financial consultant.

The owner's direction to John Read was to produce a twenty percent return on capital each year for the next five years.

John agreed that he could accomplish this results objective; and then for each one of the five years, to achieve that result, he sold off a portion of the equity of the corporation.

Obviously, this was not the intent of the owner. He had made the mistake of only having John agree to the result objective that he wanted, and not to the specific actions that he was going to take to accomplish that result.

This error in objective setting is the most common one we have found in executing the concept of O.P.E.N. Communication.

Ed Gates, Vice President of Sales of Comsigh, the computer time-sharing corporation, organizes his annual managers' meeting. At the start of the meeting, he says that his objective is to accomplish a forty percent increase in new business accounts.

Again, this is the result which Ed Gates wants, but it is not the objective for the annual business planning process.

The objective for the annual meeting is:

"To have each individual leave that meeting with a plan of action that he or she believes he or she can execute to achieve that forty percent increase in new business."

It wouldn't be feasible to talk about objectives if we didn't say a word about problems. A good definition of a problem is: "Something that stands between you and your objective." Take this a step further. If you have no objectives, you don't have any problems. Nothing is stopping you from going anywhere because you don't want to go anywhere. The reverse is true. If you don't have any problems, you don't have any objectives. You are already there.

If you stop to think about this for a minute, it will lend direction to your communications with our O.P.E.N. system. To talk about objectives without stating how you're going to solve the problems that are there would not be meaningful. For example, you say: "Smitty, how would you like $10,000 by Friday, tax free?" Smitty's reaction would probably be, "Great, but how do I get it?"

You had better be prepared to tell Smitty how he's going to get it—or to answer the question, "what problems do we have to solve by Friday in order to get it?"

Let's assume that you and Smitty own a piece of property you haven't been able to sell. You have suddenly found a buyer and solved a pre-existing problem. In short, if you hadn't had an answer to the problem, stating the objective would have been of little value.

More and more, we see why communication falls down. Our own objectives are sometimes not clear. We haven't even thought out objectives for the listener, and even if we have objectives for both parties, we haven't defined the problems, or what each must do to achieve those objectives.

There's an old definition of a fanatic: "One who, when he loses sight of his objectives, redoubles his efforts."

5
NEEDS
The Desires, Goals and Wants of People

"WINNING ISN'T EVERYTHING. IT IS THE ONLY THING." Vince Lombardi.

ACHIEVING ISN'T EVERYTHING. It is the only thing.

Why should anyone do what you want him to do? Because he wants to achieve...to achieve a personal goal, build his self-image, create a better situation for himself. If what you are asking him to do helps him achieve, then he will do it because he is *winning*, getting greater value out of the results of his actions.

That's the "N" in O.P.E.N. ... meeting the *need* the other individual has to achieve.

Let's put a handle on this complex process. Here's the situation:

> The training director of Acme Corporation has asked Don Sell to attend the class on computer systems design.

> "Don, as your record has proven, you are one of the most knowledgeable design engineers in the company. One additional area which will round out your total capacity would be the senior course in systems design."

Here we have an example of the first major category of human needs ... the need to achieve and constantly build up our own *self-image*. When Don makes the decision and takes the action to join the course, he will do so because it will enable him to grow, to deal with his environment, and to build his self-image as a real professional.

> "Don, in times past, you've told me of your personal goals to become head of the department. This senior course in systems design will be a critical step in providing you with the knowledge base necessary to achieve that position."

Here we have the second powerful human need ... the need to achieve our personal goals and objectives. Don will spend the time, energy and effort to take the course because he believes that it will assist him in *achieving* his personal goals and objectives.

> "Don, at this point, you're the only one in the department who has not successfully completed this senior course in systems design. This will probably mean that the innovative assignments won't be coming in your direction and will go to the people who have the training in advanced systems design."

Here we have the third major human need ... the need to improve upon a situation that exists today in order to achieve more tomorrow.

Don will take the action because he understands that he is not being given the creative types of assignments which he wants because he has not completed the senior course.

> "Don, although this kind of program is not one of your responsibilities today, with the combining of departments, based upon our tight economic conditions, the chances are that this will become part of the department's responsibility. With this course under your belt, you will have a real head start when the departments are combined."

Here is an example of the fourth major need ... the need to improve our situation in the future.

Don will take the course, because he believes the action requested will result in a more secure and advantageous position when the inevitable happens and the departments are combined. A need, therefore, is "a statement of a condition which an individual would want and like either now or in the future, which is different from the existing or the proposed condition." It is what the person wants to achieve. When he does achieve it, he is winning ... reaching his goals.

People will only take actions when they believe that those actions will assist them in meeting their needs.

We have identified four major categories of needs:

1. The need to enhance and build my own self-image.

2. The need to achieve my personal goals and objectives.

3. The need to improve the situation in which I'm living today.

4. My need to improve the conditions that I will be living in in the future.

The first two are dependent upon the individual's concept of himself ... self-image and personal goals and objectives. These we call personal needs.

The third and fourth categories depend upon the situation either today or in the future. In our business life, we call this "the needs for the job that I get paid to do."

As you prepare, using the discipline of O.P.E.N. Communication, you must determine what needs of the individual will be met when he or she takes the action that you want taken. Let's see what happens if we do a lousy job in clearly defining the needs of the other individual.

Charlie is a fork-lift truck operator in the Plattsberry Plant. Joe, his boss, stops him on one of his runs and says,

"Charlie, I want to change the routing that you have been using. Start with aisle #10 first, that puts the bulk items on the skid last. Okay?"

Charlie thinks to himself,

"Screw you! That's going to increase the time it takes me to make each run. That will make it harder for me to hit the standards of runs completed. That's so typical! All he wants is to look good when the inspection team comes through tomorrow."

Here we have a typical example of assuming that the other person sees the relationship between what you are asking him to do and what's in it for him if he does it.

The result of not clearly defining or communicating "what's in it for the other person" is always a deterioration of the relationship between the two individuals. It's obvious to the other person that you've really not understood his or her needs and are asking him or her to do something that will only benefit you ... not a very good way to build trust.

Let's look at the Charlie situation as it should have happened.

"Charlie, I want to change the routing that you've been using. Start with aisle #10 first, because that puts the bulk items on the skid last. If you do this, you will reduce the time you have to spend in the unloading operation and we will reduce our damage rate, which is one of the most critical factors affecting all of our incentive payments. I believe this will more than make up for the extra amount of time that it will take you on each run."

Now Charlie's reaction is:

"Hey, the boss is a pretty savvy guy! He's always looking for ways to have the job be easier and better."

The result of not determining and meeting the needs of the other person is disaster. He or she now has a living example that there is a winner and loser when he or she deals with you. The result of this attitude says, "Fool me once, shame on you. Fool me twice, shame on me." Now you've lost trust, and it will take a lot of time, energy and effort to develop your relationship to the point where the other person will again be willing to interact honestly with you.

Why is it so easy for us to forget about the other person's needs?

Ben Hogan once said, "If you do what comes naturally, you'll never play good golf."

The same holds true of selling and any other form of communication, and, by the way, any good communication should follow the accepted sales pattern. The old phrase "natural salesman" was coined in total ignorance of the sales process. It probably refers to the "hail fellow well met" attitude with a smile and back slap for everybody, which breeds as much mistrust as it ever does confidence.

Good selling, and, in our case, good communication lies in persuading someone to do something by establishing a win/win situation where there's more in it for the receiver for doing something than what he gives up to do it.

What all this means is that we become good communicators in direct proportion to how well we can understand our receiver and his or her situation and provide him or her with advantages or benefits for whatever we ask him or her to accept.

But notice something. We are not born with consideration for the other person. The psychological need for self-preservation manifests itself early in our life. The child says, "Watch me, Daddy." "Look what I drew, Mamma." I, I, I,—me, me, me. The child screams to be recognized. He knows nothing else. It's a "me" world, and that's what we're born with.

In the first stages of life, the child knows little about win/win. Even as he or she enters the teens and social need becomes a dominant factor—that is, the need to stand in with a peer group—the teen is still vying for personal attention, not thinking, "What can I do for you?"

We find that much of the success of O.P.E.N. Communication depends on shaking ourselves loose from ourselves, not "doing what comes naturally" but "doing what comes unnaturally"—stepping into the shoes of the other person.

Society aids us in viewing everything from only the self's point of view. This is done with well-meaning sayings, such as: "Do unto others as you would have others do unto you." Without any further explanation, most individuals interpret that saying as, "If I like and want it, so should you." The O.P.E.N. Communicator's interpretation is, "Make sure that what you ask the person to do meets his or her needs. Those needs are based upon the conditions the other person is living in and his or her perception of himself or herself and of his or her own goals and objectives."

This means that if we really want to understand and address the other person's needs, we must do our homework. A major guideline for this homework was given in Chapter 3, under the heading of "Self-Understanding." We should consciously look for and identify items which provide indications of self-image. The three-sided triangle and the concept of human needs provides and assists in this area.

Sometimes, needs are only emotional and maybe self-satisfying, yet they can often be just as strong as, or stronger than, highly logical and practical business needs.

A friend of mine in El Paso, Texas, was once sales manager of a large hotel and restaurant supply house. In a nearby town, a native was about to open a large restaurant which would need a great deal of equipment that my friend wanted to sell.

Being a master of win/win, he went over to this town two or three days before the bids were to be in. He walked around, conversing with people he knew and many he didn't know, always trying to find out as much about the buyer as he could. He ended up with two salient facts: one, the buyer was a tough cookie, customarily mean to salesmen, with very little patience, and strictly a dollars-and-cents business man; second, his whole life was wrapped up in his son, who was a star football player at Georgia Tech.

The day came for delivery of the contract. My friend called on Mr. Hardnose and entered his office with a bid. The buyer said he had no time for loose talk, "Just leave the bid on the pile with the others, and it better be low, or else."

As my friend turned to leave the office, he stopped for a moment and said, "Say, isn't your son the star of the Georgia Tech backfield this year?" The buyer brightened up and said, "Sure is. Have you been watching him?" My friend had done his homework. He knew the kid's record from high school on. They ended up at lunch, after which the buyer insisted they go back to his office, where he picked up my friend's bid, signed it, threw the rest in the waste basket, and said, "Deliver as soon as you can."

This is a true story. As far as I know, all characters are still alive.

But let me ask you this: suppose my friend had not done his homework? Because he was offering first class equipment, he knew his price would be among the highest. What chance would he have had to open the mind's door and establish a trusting business relationship? Recognizing Mr. Hardnose's personal needs gave him the opportunity to satisfy his business needs with products he knew would perform to the satisfaction of Mr. Hardnose—a win/win situation.

So we don't over-emphasize the emotional or self-image needs, let's look at the other side of the need coin. (Both sides exist in all of us to one degree or another.)

I was once making a call with a young salesman we had trained. The salesman was selling a popular brand of coffee, and the prospect was the owner and buyer for a chain of seven large, modern supermarkets in the Midwest. We showed up five minutes before nine o'clock, the appointment time, and sat on the mourners' bench outside the buyer's office, waiting to be called in. Before we got there, I had asked the salesman what his approach would be and what he was trying to sell, and I received a reasonable answer: "We've got 11 cents off on a can, and it's a perfect loss-leader for the buyer's stores." (A loss-leader is an offering designed to attract people to the store, which can be advertised but which returns a small, if any, profit to the store owner.)

We were finally called into the buyer's office. The buyer looked at the salesman and said, "You've got three minutes to tell me how I'm going to make money."

The salesman started out with, "We have a big promotion campaign." The buyer said, "O.K., get out—next," and he would listen no more.

The salesman was taken aback, and asked me, as we walked out, "What did I do wrong?" My answer was: "Well, not much. I guess we didn't train you very well."

In this case, the buyer had laid his needs right on the table without any shadow of doubt: "Show me how I make money," and the answer to that doesn't start with "*We have* ..." That's the natural, self-centered approach. The buyer couldn't care less about what you've got. "What's in it for me?," is his only justifiable concern.

The final outcome of this story is happier. I sat down with the salesman and said, "Let's take it from the beginning. When the buyer said, 'Show me how to make money,' you could have given him some beautiful answers that would have gone something like this: 'Sam, you make money when you get traffic through your stores. *People* is the name of your game, and your stores are new. You need a bigger chunk of the neighborhood, and I know that, and I've brought you a package that will bring 'em in off the street. You're a good merchandiser. Once you get people in, you know what to do from then on. Furthermore, the package itself is going to be a profit-maker for you. You win both ways. I can give you the details in five minutes.'"

I called back the storeowner, explained that I was trying to help this young man, and that, in fact, we really did have a good way for Sam to make money, and asked him to give the kid one more shot at laying it out for him. He agreed. The proposition was bought in its entirety, and the young man learned a lesson.

Admittedly, it's not always as easy as Sam made it. When Sam said, "Show me how to make money," there was no doubt as to where he was coming from nor what criterion he would use to judge the communication; but this incident should bring home loud and clear the precept that when the needs of the listener or receiver are clearly understood and met by the communicator, the chances of success are good.

Let's take the practical side of the needs coin a step further.

"If I am going to ask you to do something, this action must be commensurate with your responsibilities as an individual. It must enable you to accomplish those responsibilities easier, faster and better."

In other words, you will receive value in the future by taking the action, because it will enable you to control the situation and accomplish what you get paid to do.

This means that, as we prepare for an interaction using O.P.E.N., we must first understand the basic responsibility, authority, and accountability of the individual. Secondly, and more importantly, it means that we must understand the conditions under which the individual is operating today... understand his or her goals, objectives and commitments.

All of us get paid to do many things. The relative

importance of these actions (our priorities) can vary considerably, depending upon what we perceive the situation is today, and what the situation could be in the future.

Here's an example from real life. Herb Swan is a District Manager for Ajax Electric Supply Company. He has just found out that one of his major competitor's warehouses has gone out on strike. He sees this as an excellent opportunity for his company to give all the prospective customers in the marketplace a special short-term price promotion. He believes that if he does offer such a promotion, many of the customers who cannot buy the competitive product due to the warehouse strike will try his company's products. Based upon his previous experience in two other markets, he believes that fifty percent of those customers who purchase from him for the first time will continue with his company.

Herb also knows that his boss was just called on the carpet for being over budget in expense on all categories, especially the promotional expense category. In fact, just yesterday, the boss called a meeting and told all of the people that he didn't want to hear any recommendations which required an over-budget expense.

As Herb prepares for his interaction with his boss, he must consider the following items:

1. I must deal immediately with the boss's directive for no over-budget expense.

2. The boss's *immediate* need is to look good in the eyes of the corporation and control expenses. The boss's *long-term* need is to increase market share at the expense of competition and to build a volume base that allows for profit leveraging.

3. I had better be able to prove that customers who do switch from the competitor to us will, in fact, stay with us after the competitor's warehouse strike is

over. This requires drawing from our experiences in other markets where these conditions did exist, and being able to prove that fifty percent of those customers did continue to purchase.

4. I'd better cost out the exact amount of over-budget expense which will be incurred, and then calculate, based upon the estimate of fifty percent of the customers remaining with us, how long it will take not only to return that additional cost, but to generate twice that amount in extra profits.

Now, based on that type of preparation, here is the 60-second opener which Herb would use with his boss, the Regional Manager:

"Mark, I think I understand the pressure that you're operating under from corporate to reduce over-budget expense categories, and I did listen to your directive yesterday concerning over-budget expense.

"In spite of this, I'm going to ask you to approve an over-budget expense for a special three-week promotion. The purpose is to take advantage of our competitor's warehouse strike. Now, here's the plan I would like to go through with you to prove that we will return that initial investment three-fold within the first four months, and, most importantly, increase our customer base by fifteen percent.

"This will be a major step in accomplishing our primary corporate goal of increasing market-share profitability. Mark, can I have fifteen minutes to go through this plan with you?"

In this instance, the boss's initial *short-term* need was not to come in conflict with Corporate's directive to decrease over-budget expenses. The *longer term*, more overriding, and therefore, more important need on the part of the Regional Manager was to achieve the annual goals and objectives which had been established for him ... to increase share of market and meet the annual revenue objectives.

By understanding this, Herb gained his boss's understanding and then commitment to the understanding that the annual objectives were more important to him than the immediate need to reduce conflict on over-budget expenses.

Again the overriding consideration in addressing needs is to know the conditions ... all the conditions the person is living with.

What this tells us is that different people will have different needs. Needs for some simply are not needs for others. For instance, we assume that everyone wants to make money. That isn't true. Somebody once told me that Rockefeller's income was $50,000 an hour. He couldn't sleep nights because of the pressure of dispensing that kind of income. It would be an ignorant person who went to Mr. Rockefeller and said, "I'm going to show you how you can make more money."

This is an extreme example, but it makes the point. There are very few benefits that everyone in the world seeks, and those that everyone does seek are difficult to offer, like health and happiness.

And how would anyone know what would be happiness for another person? You would have to know him or her very well. Take any ten business people about to retire and ask each how he or she wants to live out the rest of his or her life. Some want to play golf, some want to fish, some to travel, some to work at what they like to do, and others just to get out of the rat race. If each were to complete his plan for the future, probably no two of the ten would be identical.

Now along comes O.P.E.N. Communication and says that any good communicator must establish a win/win situation, i.e., you must provide your receiver with an answer to his or her needs in order to get a positive response to what you are looking for, and what this chapter says is that it's not always so easy. Maybe, however, there are some approaches. Let's consider the problem/ objective approach.

We've said that a problem was anything standing between a person and his or her objectives. Practically, anyone who's alive has objectives, and the fact that he or she has not reached them yet means that there are problems. In an extreme case, maybe a person's only objective is to stay alive. If that's the case, the problem is anything that threatens his or her existence.

And if we follow our theory a step further, need only exists when a problem exists, because need is the answer to the problem. For instance, Jim Smith wants to buy a house. Jim has a good income and is not starving for money, but the house he wants requires a healthy down payment, which is ready cash he doesn't have. Jim's need is enough money to solve the down payment problem. With that problem solved, Jim reaches his objective of a new house.

Joan has completed her education in marketing and naturally wants a marketing job where she can use the capabilities she has worked for so hard. But Joan doesn't know anybody in the business world who can help her. Her problem is contacts—her need of someone who can set her up for interviews. Again, such a contact would solve the problem that stands between her and her objective.

Individuals can and should only take actions when they believe and understand that those actions will give them value in the future. Value is dependent upon a return to the individual for the time, energy, effort and risk taken when he or she does what you want him or her to do. If the action enables us to satisfy our personal needs or organization-related needs, we then say that we will be receiving value. The action will meet our needs.

The need concept is the most important of the four elements of O.P.E.N. Communication, because this is where the win/win situation is determined. Determining the needs of another individual takes considerable energy, time, effort, and desire to spend that time and energy so that we can be effective O.P.E.N. Communicators.

Achieving isn't everything...it is the only thing...for all of us. Let the other person achieve his or her goals, self-image and happiness.

6
EXPECTATIONS
Our Experience Has Become Our Jailer

Have you ever tried to learn something that, on the surface, appeared extremely simple and easy for others to master but, for some reason or other, you had trouble with? After finally learning it, you couldn't, in retrospect, fathom why it ever seemed difficult to you.

There's probably no human being who has not gone through this experience. But if, perhaps, you feel that you have not had this experience, you certainly must have seen it in others. Maybe it was only a simple goal that someone gave up on because to him or her it seemed unreachable. Or a small problem like having an acquaintance named Mary, or whatever, whom you insisted on calling Joan because Mary reminded you of a Joan you once knew.

Let's carry the above simple examples into more complicated problems, such as phobias or fears. There are all kinds of phobias: acrophobia, fear of height; aquaphobia, fear of water; sitophobia, fear of food; claustrophobia, fear of enclosure. In each of these cases something causes them, usually some bitter experience that creates a mind-set or, as some psychologists call it, an "arrested development."

We all have them, in one form or another, and they govern our lives far more than most people think. They are part of every personality. They create habits which guide our everyday life. The restaurant business suffers inordinately from them—one meal not up to par in the mind of the customer can lose that customer for life.

Personal relationships start, continue and end almost solely on this basis. A disagreeable experience with another person creates a mind-set that you may never live down.

These few examples demonstrate the tremendous influence over relationships exercised by this psychological phenomenon. Stability in people is generally characterized by a person's ability to resist the influence of a mind-set.

One doesn't have to go far to realize the devastating effect this phenomenon of mind-set has on the communication process. When you consider that relationships, whatever they may be, are only as strong as the communication between two people, we can translate the entire relationship process into one of effective or ineffective communication. Two people afraid of the dark are more likely to get along with each other than one afraid and one not afraid. The old saying "Opposites attract" is not a philosophy one can live with for any length of time. The fact that they're opposite may preclude their ever getting together in the first place. If they come together at all, it's probably because they recognize mutual interests and/or mutual friends. Once the relationship is established, it could become highly advantageous to be "opposites" in some respects, but very few people go around hoping to establish pleasant relationships with someone immediately recognizable as "not their kind."

Our jargon is filled with old saws that proclaim the other point of view:

- Birds of a feather flock together.
- The apple never falls far from the tree.
- Cut from the same cloth.

When we put ourselves in the role of engineering effective communications, and we know that defining the expectations of our receiver is important, it pays to stop for a moment and consider mind-set. As often as not, what you as an individual would value or what would be your expectations will not necessarily match those of your receiver.

Let's look at an example. Over the last thirty years of working with individuals from hundreds of companies, I've heard this remark from subordinates: "It doesn't do any good for me to take my ideas in to the boss. It's virtually an automatic turn-down, and he looks at me as if I had just stepped off a space ship. I quit trying to be creative a long time ago. I just let him run the business, and I go along with whatever he wants to do. It's easier."

Then we go to the other side, the boss: "I get tired of half-baked ideas. I don't want to discourage the people who report to me, but I would just once like to see a proposition laid on my desk with all the facts. I don't know what they expect. They come in with a new idea. They haven't researched it. What do they want me to do? If I had to go out and gather the facts and make decisions on all the ideas that have been thrown on my desk over the years, I wouldn't have any time to run the business."

This is a classic example of a dichotomy where neither side considered the expectations of the other.

Let's see how it might work—and I can do it best with a true story.

I was once sales manager of a good-sized operation. It was just after World War II, and the only reason I was sales manager was because there wasn't anybody else. I was terribly guilty of the "half-baked idea" syndrome. I would throw some strange-looking propositions on the desk of my boss, but my boss was far smarter than I and knew a lot more about expectations. He recognized my weaknesses, my expectations and my needs. He also knew I wasn't going to get any better without some help.

He would regard one of these brainstorms very seriously, and then say, "What are you doing tonight after dinner? Why don't we meet here in my office and go over this."

When we met, he would show me how to develop that proposition, how to get the facts on it, and what the problems were that might arise, and how to weigh them against the benefits that would accrue. He would show me how to research the facts and how the proposal might be sold to supreme headquarters. We might work far into the night. Then he would say, "O.K., now take the proposition back, and when you've got in into shape, if you still think it's a good idea, maybe it is."

We didn't have too many of those sessions, and how much he helped me cannot be measured.

There are those who point out that not everybody is willing to take all that time. Take all that time? He saved thousands of hours for every one he spent. True, he got back only a fourth of the ideas originally laid on his desk, but when they were put there, he could tell in five minutes whether they were worth doing or not, and they usually were.

I shudder to think of what would have happened to me in business without that kind of a boss early in the game. If he had simply ignored my suggestions or criticized me for bringing them in or ridiculed them in any way, he would have created a negative mind-set, and we both would have been losers.

There are times when the mind-set is so strong that you can't break through it. The human being is an animal, albeit an advanced animal, and the animal traits are there. We can see the same thing in dogs. If you kick a young dog often enough, he will cower at the approach of any human and avoid contact. Communication with the dog becomes virtually impossible.

Psychological problems with humans can be far more subtle, but those of us who would communicate effectively must be aware that they are there and that until they are dealt with, effective communication is not possible. People don't always wear those problems out in the open. So the more we can learn about someone prior to the communication effort, or the more we do our homework, the better chance we have of establishing a win/win relationship.

The "E" in O.P. E.N. forces us to do our homework. We live in the world of other people. What they do has an immediate effect upon us, and conversely, our actions have an immediate effect upon others.

> Let us imagine that you are standing in a room with your eyes closed. Nobody else is in the room. Somebody brings me into the room with my eyes closed and stands me facing you. He then leaves. You know absolutely nothing about me — names, title, job, experiences — and I know nothing about you. We are total strangers. Now the only muscles we both use simultaneously is to open our eyes. The very instant that you open your eyes and get a picture of me that picture will go into your computer mind against all the experiences that you have had with people that look like me, stand like me and act like me. This instantaneous recognition will immediately start to affect your thought processes and your emotions.

> As a result of this instantaneous thought process, we start to act. If my image of you elicits experiences that have been friendly and positive, I'll immediately smile and reach out my hand to shake yours. The almost instantaneous tendency on your part, observing my actions, is to respond in a similar way. You then smile and reach out your hand to shake mine.

> If, however, your experiences say that people who look like me have been suspicious, didn't want to be involved and had resisted friendly overtures, then you'd probably take a slight step backward and look defensive. My tendency then would be to react in the

same way and ask the questions, "Who are you? ... What are you doing here?" In turn, your reaction to this could be, "Who wants to know?" ... and so on.

We intuitively respond (change our actions) to the perceived actions and intent of the other person. This interpretation or filtering of the looks, actions and words of the other person is determined by the experiences that we've had before ... for example, our reaction to a person with a scar on his face or one who uses incorrect grammar. Most importantly, our reaction will probably show in our own actions.

Expectation means that every time two people come face to face, they bring three levels of awareness based upon their experiences.

The **first** level of expectation is my understanding and feeling about *myself* in this interaction.

The **second** level of expectation is *my perception* of the type of *person that you are,* and therefore what I can expect you to do, think and feel.

The **third** level of expectation is what I believe the *situation* is going to call for during this interaction.

Let's look at a typical, real-life example. The situation is one which we have observed many times.

We have been asked by a major corporation to design and develop a training program for their purchasing agents. In order to determine the exact skill needs of these purchasing agents, we must sit in their offices and observe them with various salespeople. The objective is to determine exactly what is their analytical capacity, decision-making capacity, and capacity to use all the skills of communication, such as listening, responding, fact-gathering, etc., so that we can design a meaningful training program.

Here's what happens:

Salesperson #1 comes in. You don't even have to look at the buyer. You observe the actions of the salesperson and it is obvious that he has an image of the buyer. This person believes that the buyer wants all the details, and wants those details laid out in order succinctly, leaving nothing out.

Now, it must be obvious that *good* salespeople react and respond differently to different buyers. Buyers are also people who must live in the world of others. They, too, respond and react differently to different salespersons.

The result of the interaction above was a very pedantic and methodical, metronome type of reaction.

Now, Salesperson #1 gets up and leaves. In comes Salesperson #2. Again, you don't even have to watch the actions of the buyer. As you observe the words and actions of Salesperson #2, it is obvious that this individual has a different concept of the buyer. Salesperson #2 believes the buyer wants only the top-line facts, and wants them laid out succinctly and rapidly.

Amazingly, as you observe, the buyer reacts to this salesperson in a very rapid-fire way.

The key point: The way an individual acts with you one-on-one is not necessarily the way he acts with any other individual one-on-one. It is based on what he has learned to do with you as a result of what you have done to him. That's the result of *expectation* and experience.

What does this mean and do to communications? Let's come back and look at the three levels of expectation which each individual brings to every communication.

Expectation Level #1: What I expect of me.

Each of us has a very complex set of self-images. These self-images, in any given period of time, have a tremendous effect on how we respond to any given situation. For example, if my self-esteem is at a high at a particular moment and I feel confident, feel that I am in control of my environment, this will enable me to look at the actions of others with sharper objectivity.

Conversely, if I am concerned, in a high state of anxiety, and come face to face with another individual, the chances are my actions will be defensive and thus not allow me to listen to and react to the other person objectively.

Here's a situation:

A salesperson is about ready to walk into his customer's conference room to make the final presentation to the operating committee for the decisions on his company's product. Just before he enters the conference room, the secretary calls him over to answer the telephone. The individual picks up the telephone and it is his Vice President of Sales. The Vice President chews him out for losing a major customer due to his errors. The salesperson knows that he was wrong and even stupid.

He now hangs up the phone and walks into the conference room to make the presentation to the operating committee. Obviously, his actions are going to be affected, based upon the image that he has of himself walking into that room. He will not exude the type of confidence with which he had prepared his presentation.

Now, let's take the same circumstances, but this time when the secretary calls him over to answer the telephone, it is the Vice President of Sales, telling him that the approach that he took to their largest customer broke a major deadlock and they were now the sole supplier to that company.

Now, the salesperson hangs up the phone and walks into make his major presentation. Obviously, his self-confidence and his image of his capacity to interact objectively in this new meeting will be considerably different.

Here we've seen some examples of the first level of expectation which controls to a considerable extent the actions that we will take in any given interaction. Most importantly, the other individual in this interaction will see our actions—the indicators of how we feel about ourselves—and will respond accordingly.

Expectation Level #2: ... What I expect of you.

Every one of us has an image of the people that we deal with. This image has been created through the experiences that we've had with those individuals. Go back to the example where we had never met the individual before, knew absolutely nothing about him or her. The sheer picture that we get of that individual will elicit a reaction on our part, based upon the experiences we've had with individuals who look, stand, and act in the same way.

The important consideration is that the image I have of another person affects my actions with that individual. This image immediately affects us in two ways:

1. It causes us to filter out any words or actions other than those that we are preconditioned to see and hear.

2. It will cause us to take actions which are consistent with our image of the other person.

In most instances, we do not come face to face with an individual without some previous knowledge or experience with that person.

Those experiences have caused us to develop a mental profile of that person. That profile now determines the kind of person we believe he is, what his decisions will be, what his skills are, his communication capacity, and his self-image.

Now, this profile acts just like a filter on a camera, which only allows those shades of light and color to come through which are consistent with the profile that we have developed of the individual.

Here's an example:

Joe Murphy has been known both to cut corners on his expense account, and to report to his management only the positive information concerning the conditions in his territory. Joe now requests an increase in his expense budget. The request is based upon a realistic, well thought out, and justifiable analysis of his situation. The boss's profile of Joe, however, let's him hear only those slight miscommunications and hesitancies which say to him, "No, no, this is not a reasonable request!"

Here is another example:

A National Sales Manager and his five Regional Managers were reviewing the 23 District Managers across the country for promotion. As soon as the discussion came to the District Manager in San Francisco, there was an immediate reaction from the National Sales Manager. The comment was, "I knew it! Last week, Harry started acting like a New Yorker in that San Francisco market."

Now, here are the actual facts of the situation. Harry had been in the San Francisco market for four years, had had a greater increase in sales volume than any other District Manager in the country, and had had more people promoted out of his district than any other District Manager. Yet the National Sales Manager was not concerned with these facts. He had a preconceived idea, an image of the kind of person Harry was, and as soon as one action was taken which reconfirmed that preconceived idea, the next comment of the Manager was, "It was really only a question of time."

In the above situation, we have a sample of a condition called prejudgment ... prejudice. This means we have established a profile, an image, of the type of person we believe the other individual to be. And this image then filters out all communication from the individual that is not consistent with our preconceived idea of that person.

Unfortunately, we all have hundreds of prejudgments that affect our relationships with people. When this condition exists, we must understand it and deal with it in our preparation and execution of the interaction with the other individual if our communication is to be effective.

Expectation Level #3: The situation or the environment.

People do not interact in a vacuum. They interact in a specific environment, or situation. Our expectation of what we believe this situation calls for again has considerable impact on the action that we will take.

Two friends meet in front of a church at an appointed hour. In one instance, it is to go in for a funeral. In another instance for a wedding. The actions of both individuals will be considerably different based upon the expectation of the situation.

Most readers can probably think of an example of an individual who is really fun to be with when he or she is away from the office, but who is insufferable in the environment of the business. This happens because the individual has a concept, an expectation of how he or she believes he or she should act in the business environment.

In Summary

The expectation concept establishes the fact that each individual in an interaction brings three levels of expectation to that interaction. The first is the image that I have of myself. The second is the image that I have of the other person. The third is my understanding of what the situation actually calls for.

The first critical point is that those expectations will:

1. Cause me to alter my initial actions with the other individual.

2. Cause me to filter out what is actually happening based upon my expectations.

The "E" in O.P.E.N. Communication (expect) therefore reminds us to understand, recognize and take into consideration this concept.

The expectation must be considered from two time-frame perspectives:

1. What the experience expectations will be of both individuals coming into this interaction ... this is the "where are you coming from?"

2. The definition of the roles that each one of us should play during the interaction, in order to insure that our actions will not cause the other to become defensive. The roles that each will play must be understood by each, so that there is agreement on what we can expect of each other and what the situation is calling for.

When both of these time-frames of expectation are dealt with in our preparation for the interaction, we have taken a major step toward achieving win/win, the structure of insuring understanding.

When the expectation concept is not understood and addressed in the preparation, start, and execution of interactions with people, the tendency is for individuals to become defensive. All the blocks to understanding caused by our previous experience and conditioning now come into play. People don't actually see or hear the other person, so there is no understanding. This immediately becomes evident to the other person, which proves to him or her, "You are not interested in me, only in yourself. Therefore, I'd better not trust you with a real understanding of my thoughts and feelings."

The result is energy is spent by both people in playing games. Value is lost. There is little understanding. Mistakes occur. Now both will have the tendency to protect themselves at the expense of the other person.

By understanding, identifying and preparing for our experience filters, we can defuse the emotional blocks and deal objectively together. That's the "E" in O.P.E.N.

7
PLANNING
The Road Map to Agreement

PLAN... A DIRTY FOUR LETTER WORD!

The truth of the matter is that people don't like to create a plan. This statement is borne out by all of the research on attitudes of business people toward the science of management.

We recently polled over 3,000 salespeople. One of the questions asked people to indicate the most important ingredients for success in selling. The result, by almost unanimous agreement, was that success element Number One was "know the needs of your customer ... Amen." Success element Number Two was planning. Plan your work and work your plan. If you are going to be successful in selling, this is an absolute must.

Now comes the interesting part. When the same 3,000 people were asked, "Do you actually create a plan for your territory or your business?," *only* ten percent said "Yes."

What causes this dichotomy? From in-depth interviews the reasons for the tremendous inconsistency between actions on planning and the attitude about the importance of planning came out loud and clear. "Planning causes me to lose control. It becomes a straitjacket. I need to be able to react to the situation. If I try to execute the plan the way I set it up, it won't work and I'll lose control."

The truth of the matter is that the only way you can control anything is to have a plan. Now you know what you want to deviate from. Without that plan, you must be reactionary. When you are reactionary, you have lost control.

Project *Mariner*, which sent our spacecraft to Mars, was a ten-year planning project. There were more than 16,000 sequential planning steps through all the system. Yet, seven seconds after the buttons were pushed to send that rocket off the face of the earth, the first adjustment was made to that ten-year plan. Before Mariner landed on Mars, over 4,000 adjustments had been made to the original plan.

The average person, looking at the number of adjustments, says, "Why waste all that time on planning? Let's just push the buttons and play it by ear."

Obviously, Mariner would never have landed on Mars if this "no planning" policy had been followed. Maybe not so obviously, you can't achieve any of your objectives unless you start with a plan that you want to use to get there.

But you must also recognize that you must adjust that plan. To do this, the planning process you use must allow for that adjustment.

One of the major reasons why people do not create a plan is that they don't know the difference between planning *as a process* and the document which is the result of that process, *called a plan*. The second major reason is that they really don't know how to plan. We assume that as a spider comes into the world knowing how to spin a web, so are people born with the innate capacity to plan. Nothing could be further from the truth.

Let's examine the *planning process* as it is applied to controlling our interactions with other people, communication. The four elements of O.P.E.N. provide the structure for planning. When these four elements are considered and then integrated in the preparation phase of O.P.E.N.

Communication, we insure that the planning process has started, and that we will be able to create a plan which both of us can use to arrive at a mutually beneficial decision ... win/win.

Wait a minute: we said the only way you can control anything is to have a plan, because now you know what you want to deviate from. This is the first time that we've heard that word "control" in relation to the process of O.P.E.N. Communication. Control what and for whose benefit?

The most important person to control is yourself. When you lose control of yourself, you lose. Remember the freeway fender-bender example that we gave? Without the "mind-set" of the discipline of O.P.E.N. Communication, the natural tendency of all of us is to attack, to defend ourselves with any logical or illogical approach. This immediately forces the other person to become defensive and he or she attacks. The result is a lose/lose situation. By preparing for the interaction with O.P.E.N. Communications, we can control our own mind-set, our own emotions. This then sets the stage for the other person to recognize that this is not an attack situation. The result is that our time is spent in trying to understand and to reach mutually beneficial decisions. The result is the development of a high trust level.

Control also applies to the communication process itself. We have already seen numerous examples of the "flying by the seat of your pants," undisciplined approach to interaction between people. It usually results in miscommunication, then misunderstanding, then mistrust. Time is wasted. Mistakes are made. Then we wonder what went wrong.

This leads to the second concern about control ... control for whose benefit? For the benefit of both of us. Our intent is to reach win/win, because that is the only kind of condition that we can both live with in the future. I am not trying to control you, neither do I want you to control me.

The plan, therefore, becomes a road map which both

of us use in order to reach mutually beneficial objectives. It is the road map that I will share with you to make sure that you will achieve a win. It is not a cleverly devised scheme to control your thoughts and emotions.

By practicing the 60-second opener and sharing the plan with the other person, the plan then becomes the control.

The actual plan or road map cannot be established until we've first done our homework. We then have inter-related our objectives with the needs of the other person, based upon the conditions under which we will both be living. O.P.E.N., therefore, provides the structure for our planning process.

The Normal Steps in the O.P.E.N. Communication Plan

Our communication plan always starts with the 60-second opener. The purpose of the 60-second opener is to establish a mind-set, a mental attitude on the part of the other individual, which says, "I'm willing to listen and interact with you." Its purpose is to eliminate the possible blocks which might immediately occur which would get in the way of understanding. Remember, communication is a vehicle by which people interact. The structure of that vehicle, there-fore, is critical to insuring that the communication process will take place. By executing the 60-second opener, we are accomplishing a number of things.

1.   We are telling the other person the results of all of our preparation for this interaction.

2.   We prove that we have prepared for the interac-tion.

3.   We prove our concern for the other person's needs, by stating those needs up front.

4.   We establish the base for a trust level by telling the other person exactly what action we are going to ask him or her to take.

5. We're indicating our willingness to put everything out on the table by dealing with expectations based upon previous experience.

6. We are laying out the ground rules under which
   both of us should be operating in order to insure
   a balance of control.

7. We're indicating the plan we would like both of us
   to use to determine if, in fact, we have a win/win
   situation.

It is important to note that we do not go into the plan in
any detail in the 60-second opener. We must merely indicate by showing the outline or the agenda that we, in fact,
do have a plan. You can't go into any element of the *plan*
because it causes evaluative thinking on the part of the
receiver. You don't want evaluation at this time. Remember, the purpose of the 60-second opener is to get as a
mental attitude, "I'm willing to communicate openly with
you to see if this is a win/win situation."

The second step in the plan is the same in all interactions. You must **get, receive,** and **respond** to the feedback
of the other individual. Those three words, *get* (elicit),
receive and *respond,* spell out what is meant by *double
feedback.*

The 60-second opener is a broadcast. Communication
as defined in Chapter 3 has not occurred until there is
feedback. This insures that there is understanding ... not
just of the words but of the ideas, the intent behind the
words; and willingness to continue with the interaction in
an open, objective and honest way (not playing games or
becoming defensive).

Look at the first element of the double feedback ... *get*
feedback. Remember, the intent of the 60-second opener
was to establish a positive mind-set. After broadcasting,
you do not know the mind-set of the other person. You do
know, however, that he or she has filtered that broadcast
through all of his or her experiences *and* expectations of
this situation. You must, therefore, receive a feedback
which indicates:

- That the other person understands the action that you are going to ask him or her to take at the end of the session.

- That there is agreement on the needs that you have assumed that the other individual has.

- That emotions stemming from past experiences and/or present expectations are addressed and eliminated, so that they will not become a block.

- That the individual feels comfortable with the rules by which both play, and the plan of communication which both will use.

An individual cannot go with the rest of the plan until those first conditions have been satisfied. It would be like having a pot-bellied stove in the middle of winter which we are trying to fire up. We can throw all the coal that we want to at that pot-bellied stove, but if the door is not open, not too much heat will be generated.

People's minds are the same way. They must be open and willing to communicate to reach understanding. Until this is accomplished, it is senseless to go on with the communication.

In getting feedback, we must make sure that the individual is responding to all of the above conditions. This does not mean that we should ask for and receive a commitment of understanding on all of those items separately.

This is where the second element of double feedback comes into play... *receiving* the feedback. Remember, the intent of the 60-second opener is to establish a positive mind-set. This means that as we are receiving the feedback from the other individual, we must receive his or her *attitudes and emotions*.

Attitudes, feelings and emotions are most evident in the use of an individual's voice and in his or her body actions. As you receive the feedback, be conscious of the tone of voice, the inflections, and the rate of the verbal feedback. Listen with your eyes to the body actions of the other individual to determine if the positive mind-set has been established.

Normally, if the positive mind-set has not been established, the individual will, not just with his or her voice and body actions, but with words, indicate that there is a problem.

Let's go back to where we looked at the fender-bender example on the Ventura Freeway. It was obvious that the emotional state of the individual would not allow any objective of meaningful interaction which would result in a win/win situation.

When this is the case, we have now established how we must *respond* to that feedback ... the third element of the double feedback concept. The first "no-no" is to place blame for emotion on the other individual. The second "no-no" is to attempt to take the emotion away from the other individual. You cannot argue or order emotion out of existence.

One of the approaches to handling the highly emotional reaction is to go back and restate your 60-second opener, as was done in the example of the fender-bender.

In most of our interactions in life, there are more complex issues at stake. The result will be that the person will zero in on either the objective, the need or the expectation as being the critical element which is blocking his or her willingness to go on with the interaction. Now you must deal with the substance of that particular block.

Mary Dobbins was a long-time employee at a government agency. Through the years, her last boss had allowed her to make final decisions on the cost budgets of the various departments under this agency.

Ted Jones, the new agency manager, felt that this was an element of his responsibility and authority which he could not delegate to Mary and still control the agency himself.

Here's Ted's 60-second opener with Mary:

"Mary, it is very important for both of us to know and understand the areas of responsibility and authority that we will have as we work together running this department. I believe that there might be a feeling of possible loss of control on your part. What we should accomplish today is to gain an understanding of the specific level of authority each one of us will have in establishing the budget for the departments. Here is a step-by-step plan that I would like us both to go through to arrive at that decision."

Response from Mary:

"Do you mean to say that you are going to take away all my authority so that I go back to being a rubber stamp?"

Here we have an indication that the specific objective of the interaction was not understood, and that Mary is emotionally upset about the fact that she is reporting to a new boss with new rules.

The response to finish the double feedback on the part of the boss could be:

"Mary, there are a lot of defined areas where you have both the authority and responsibility for actions. The area that I would like to discuss and reach agreement on today concerns only approval of over-budget expenses on the part of our Department Managers."

Now, if Mary's response is one that indicates a positive mind-set, such as: "I think it is very important that we both understand what we can and can't do," then the manager can continue with the rest of the plan.

Remember, the 60-second opener is not to attempt to get the individual to agree to take the action, but to agree to interact objectively to determine whether it will be a win/win situation.

Mary's response might be still emotional, indicating a block to continuing the discussion:

"Look, I've seen seven bosses come and go on this job, and I know the pattern. Take away all the accountability and authority and just make the person a robot."

Then Ted's response should again deal with the emotion of the individual *but* not place blame. He probably would say:

"I think I can understand why you feel that way; but if we can go through this planned agenda, perhaps you will see by my actions and by the decisions we will both make that this is not the case at all."

Now, if Mary's response is:

"Okay, as long as you don't have a closed mind to it. You know I have been around here for a long period of time" ...

then the manager can continue with his plan.

Double feedback indicates that you, the initiator, must get the other individual to tell you how he or she feels about what you have just communicated. In the 60-second opener, you have communicated an objective, his or her needs, and the expectation, and indicated the plan you would like both of you to follow. Therefore, the feedback you are requesting is an honest interaction as to how the other person feels about any part or all of that 60-second opener.

If the response you get to a 60-second opener is merely okay, and you've listened to the okay with your ears, and you've observed the body action of the individual with your eyes, and there seems to be some indication that it is really not okay, then your response back should be:

"So that I understand ... what really are you saying okay to?"

Now, if you've misread the individual, he or she will come back with, "No, it really is okay. Go on!" If you have not misread, the chances are the individual will start to talk about what is on his or her mind that will block his or her willingness and capacity to interact openly and honestly.

For example, going back to the Mary situation, Mary might have said, "Sure, that's okay. Dictate, you're the boss, but that doesn't mean I really have to like it!"

Now, we have the emotion and the block out on the table, which is where it must be in order for us to deal with it effectively.

We have now covered the first two steps of the plan, which are always consistent and always used when one is practicing O.P.E.N. Communication. The exact sequence of the next series of steps in the plan will vary considerably, depending upon the purpose of the interaction.

These steps should include:

1. Establishing and gaining agreement on the facts of the situation.

2. Gaining agreement on the relationship between the facts and the ideas as they are discussed.

3. Establishing proof that if the individual does take the action you want him or her to take, that it will result in his or her receiving benefit.

4. Applying the principle of double feedback constantly to insure that the communication process is occurring and that both of you are listening not only for words but to the feelings and meanings behind those words. These double feedback sessions are called *reality checks*. We cannot assume that just because both individuals started with the willingness to interact openly, that something hasn't happened which has caused the individual to feel defensive, and thus close the mind to understanding.

5. The last step is always a mutual commitment to action.

Now, you can say, "Wait a minute, this is the first time that I've heard of mutual commitment to a course of action."

Let's go back and look at our definition of win/win. We have a win/win situation when both individuals receive a greater benefit than the cost of taking the action (or the risk involved in taking the action). The benefit to be derived, therefore, is in the future. It is rarely at the exact moment that we are interacting.

Now, if we really believe in the concept of win/win, this says that *we* must also take some action to insure that the other person will, in fact, receive the benefits. In O.P.E.N. Communication we say that the intent and purpose is to be able to live with the other person in the future with the actions that *both* of use are taking today. I must make a commitment to you to take specific actions to make sure that you will receive the value promised.

One of the cardinal laws of selling is "never let a sale end without promising to do something for the buyer."

The promise might be to check on a delivery schedule and telephone the buyer back to insure that the product will be delivered on time. The most insecure time for all buyers is the span between the decision to take an action and the actual delivery and use of the product and service. Don't let that person feel alone during that critical time period. Do something and communicate to prove your concern and desire for positive results.

Here are some check points to consider to insure that your plan from Step 3 on through to the last step will be effective and efficient:

1. The steps must be consistent with the rules established during the 60-second opener. For example, let's say you've established that this is *your* decision to make based upon your authority. You are only asking for the *counsel* and *advice* of the other person. Then don't switch roles half-way

through the plan and ask the individual to tell you what to do.

If a manager has established the purpose of a meeting as mutual problem-solving, and indicated that the consensus of the group will decide, then he mustn't switch roles half-way through and exercise an executive prerogative by saying, "It's my decision and I'll make it."

2. The plan must allow for both persons to bring their previous experience with the issue to bear on the situation. When this happens, don't be surprised if the other individual has had different types of experiences from yours. This must be expected. When this happens, don't become defensive. That would stop the communication process and stop understanding. Recognize the situation for what it is. We are different people with our own experiences as our teacher. Examine those experiences in the light of the objectivity of today's situation and conditions. Remember that the other individual must feel comfortable with *and* own the decision he or she makes. To do this, the person must feel comfortable with the fact that this situation is different from the experiences that he or she has already had. This cannot be accomplished by saying that his or her experience was wrong, or trying to prove that that experience was wrong. The important thing is to identify the *conditions* that existed when that experience happened, then explain the differences in the conditions that exist today or will exist in the future.

3. As you start to execute your plan, remember that it is a *road map*. It is not a straitjacket. The chances are you will have to deal with the feelings and ideas and experiences of the other person as you start to get feedback and deal with the real issues.

These are the side-trips that are absolutely necessary in order to continue an open dialogue. The plan when used as a road map, however, always brings you back to the mainstream of the logical thought process to arrive at a beneficial decision.

4. The steps in the plan should enable you to *reach understanding* before you press for agreement or decision making. This is stated so easily. It's amazing how we attempt to reach agreement before understanding has been reached. The plan should form the stepping-stones to agreement. By having the plan outlined, on a piece of paper or a chart, both parties can insure that understanding is being attained at each step of the way. When we then come to the final step, a mutual commitment to a course of action, the ownership for that decision then rests on both parties.

If the other person says, "As a result of our discussion, I have determined the best course of action for me to take is ... ," this indicates ownership of the decision. The poor way to have any session end, is "You've convinced me. I'll take the action you want me to take."

In this instance, there is no ownership. When problems arise—and Murphy's Law is bound to apply, and some little thing will get screwed up—if there is no ownership, the other person will then place the blame on you for the decision.

If the other person owns the decision himself, then he will understand that little things can go wrong and will work his way through those things, so that the main objective can be achieved.

In a structured organization, there are a number of reasons why people get together. A person does not have to reinvent the wheel every time a particular purpose for an interaction arises.

Managers are called upon to play many roles during the execution of their management responsibility ... roles such as:

Directing
Teaching
Coaching
Motivating
Mutual problem-solving
Performance reviews
Conflict management
Recommending
Counselling
Negotiating

In each one of these roles, there is a well-established, defined sequence of action ... a plan, which both parties can follow to insure a successful conclusion to that type of interaction.

It is not the intent in this book to define, explain and develop an understanding of each one of these roles. To do so would require ten additional chapters.

The point is that they all involve common sense. By following the discipline of O.P.E.N. in all three phases (preparation, 60-second opener, and execution of the plan), an individual will develop his or her commonsense approach to each individual role.

One final observation on planning. We started with the thesis that the purpose of planning is to control, and that the result of planning is a documented plan which, in fact, is a road map. One of the best ways to get totally detoured from that road map is to use *absolutes*.

"There is no other way." "This is the only item to be considered." "This is not open for discussion."

These statements indicate a closed mind. They also put the receiver in a corner. There are no options. No room for discussion. It makes the receiver feel that he or she has lost control. These are the tactics of the closed communicator.

It is amazing how our habit patterns of using absolutes have been developed. You must be confident. You must state your position positively. But these things can be accomplished easily *without* using absolutes.

Planning is another one of those talents we call "natural." By following the guidelines in this chapter, you will develop the *skill* of planning for the most important aspect of your life ... communicating with people.

8
WHO'S IN CONTROL

"Will I lose control of the situation if I'm dealing with a closed communicator...a power oriented person? I mean, this whole process seems too open...too naive."

"Let's face it, my boss is a closed communicator. He believes in winning through intimidation. If I try this O.P.E.N. approach, I'll be taken to the cleaners."

These are the greatest concerns most people have at this stage in their understanding of the structure of O.P.E.N. Communication.

The answer is simple, the person who:

- *Believes* he or she is in control
- *Allows* the other person to be in control

is in control.

Now, you might say, "Wait a minute, it seems like you're starting to switch horses. You said that the objective and philosophy behind O.P.E.N. Communication was win/win. Now you're saying that the individual who believes the he or she is in control, is in control. Isn't that the power approach?"

Well…the question is, *in control of what?* The person who believes that he or she is in control of himself or herself in fact *is* in control of himself or herself.

The second part of our simple answer was, "allow the other person to be in control … of himself or herself." Remember, we are not establishing a contest or a war. We don't want people to become defensive or insecure; neither do *we* want to become defensive or insecure.

One of the tactics a closed communicator uses is to get you off-balance, put you in a negative, defensive position, make you feel insecure. In that way, he will be able to control you.

The underlying philosophy behind O.P.E.N. Communication is, "I must be in control of myself, but I do not necessarily have to control you in order to do this."

This says that in all interactions there is a *power base* … not a power struggle between two individuals. It is important to remember in win/win that the first winning is my winning. I must achieve my needs, my goals, my desires, because my life is critical to me.

This does not mean, however, that I must do this at your expense. Quite to the contrary. It means that the only way long-term trust relationships are built, and the way that we continue to achieve our objectives with the minimum loss of effort is for me to allow you to achieve what you want.

O.P.E.N. Communication is proactive, not reactive. It is a vehicle for the person who wants to achieve. It is the most powerful method of realizing achievement. But this does not happen at the expense of other people.

The underlying purpose behind O.P.E.N. Communication is to build the power of both individuals. Not power over other people's actions, but power over our own actions.

Hundreds of books have been written on the sources of power. A person can achieve power through knowledge and skills. He or she can gain power through association with others in power. He or she can gain power legally or by virtue of being elected.

But the most awesome source of power is **personal power.**

The famous leaders of all times, *all* had personal power. They were strong people. Strong in their belief in themselves. Unwavering in their loyalty to an idea. Absolutely confident in their capacity eventually to succeed.

The O.P.E.N. Communicator can and must develop this source of power. The structure of O.P.E.N. Communication gives us the steps to develop that power. By establishing objectives for each interaction, it forces us to be goal-oriented, to determine what we want to accomplish with our lives. This is a major ingredient of personal power.

We must create the plan. To do this, we must become effective planners and understand the planning process, which is another key ingredient of personal power.

By concentrating on the needs of others, we insure the development of a high trust level. With this trust level comes loyalty ... again, another ingredient of personal power.

There we have briefly the first three elements of the four parts of O.P.E.N. Communication...the *objective*, the *plan*, and the *need*. The last part is *expectation* ... understanding of what kind of person we are dealing with.

This leads us back to the concern stated at the start of this chapter... "will I lose if I'm dealing with a practiced, avowed, closed communicator?"

To understand this situation, we must first define the difference in the philosophies, the beliefs behind these two diametrically opposed approaches to communication.

The closed communication approach had a surge of popularity in the 1970s and '80s. More than a hundred books have been written that espouse this philosophy ... Michael Korda's book *POWER*, and Ralph Ringer's *WINNING THROUGH INTIMIDATION*, for example. In terms of getting their message, if you've read one, you've read them all. The message is this: "All interactions between people are power struggles and there will be a winner and a loser."

The belief is that in all interactions there is a pie which is going to be divided between two individuals. Because the pie is finite, if I get a larger piece, that means that you get a smaller piece.

Ringer uses the analogy of poker chips, where each individual comes into an interaction with a set of poker chips. At the end, somebody is going to walk away with the other person's poker chips.

The O.P.E.N. philosophy says:

"Each individual has the capacity to assist the other in achieving his or her objectives."

This says that the world doesn't consist of interactions where pies are constantly being cut up, but that each of us can add value to our relationship with another. In fact, it is only as we do this that we both grow. Relationships are not finite. They are infinite. The capacities for individuals to grow constantly and add value is tremendous.

Our philosophy really is our internal guidance system. This guidance system determines the actions that we will take in any given situation. In order to understand how to win in relationship with the closed communicator, we must take actions that protect our *rights*.

Each one of us has rights and nobody should be able to take those rights away. The one person I have to live with constantly in the future is myself. I must be concerned about my rights because if I lose them, I will be living with the loss of those rights for a long period of time. In the interaction between people, what you do affects me and what I do affects you. With this understanding, I must prepare for all interactions so that I will not lose my rights. The process of O.P.E.N. Communication in preparation insures that this will not happen. Again, it is a proactive approach, not a reactive approach.

Most importantly, in protecting my rights, I do not have to take your rights away from you. If I attempt to do so, I'm really establishing the rules of war, when now we're both going to have to spend energy *against* each other.

This is energy we can't spend to insure that the future will meet both our needs. The whole process of O.P.E.N. in preparation insures that this won't happen.

We all have many rights as human beings. The intent of this chapter is not to deal with all of those rights, but to define the method by which you can protect those rights. Once you understand the method, you can then apply this to every right which is threatened.

Remember, the closed communicator wants to control you. To do this, he must make you give up your rights. He uses manipulative techniques that cause you to give up those rights.

To avoid this and gain control, you *merely* have to recognize and identify the technique. A manipulative technique, once recognized for what it is, has no effect.

Then, you must restate your right to set the power stage correctly. Let's look at a specific example.

Ted Evens is Manager of Administration of Seabring Tube. One of his responsibilities is to insure that deviations from pricing policy are identified and controlled.

Chuck McCulloch is Product Manager for the flexible tube line. Both Ted and Chuck report to Ray Thompson, Vice President of Marketing. They are also both in line to be his replacement when Ray retires in three years.

Chuck drops by Ted's office one morning:

CHUCK: Hi, Ted. How are things going?

TED: Okay! What brings you down to the third floor?

CHUCK: Well, I have a concern that some of the policies of the company are not being adhered to by the guys in sales. You know, letting customers know ahead of time about price change dates so that they can buy in.

I really can understand that in today's marketplace and with the squeeze in pressure for volume, how that type of thing could be happening.

To be honest with you I had some difficulty with my own people on all of the policy changes we've just gone through. Ted, what do you think is really happening in sales?

TED: Well, I really don't know. But now that you've mentioned it, I guess the opportunity is there. Every once in a while I, too, get an uncomfortable feeling in my gut about what is really happening out there with the customer.

(With that, Ray Thompson walks past Ted's office and Chuck calls for him to come in.)

CHUCK: Say, Ray, remember our conversation this morning. Ted here just admitted that there probably are advance communications on our pricing increase going to our customers by field sales.

TED: Wait a minute! I didn't say that. I said that they have the opportunity.

CHUCK: Yes, and then you admitted that you do have uneasy feelings.

RAY: Now hold on a minute, Ted. Dammit, we pay you to make damn sure that our pricing policies are followed up. Our edge in the marketplace is critical to us. I don't want any uneasy feelings from you. I want you be on top of your job.

There we have a prime example of one of the most blatant manipulative techniques.

The closed communicator will volunteer a piece of confidential information about himself, his history or his thoughts. He now believes he has total justification for asking you to give him a piece of confidential or private information about yourself. Then once he has this information, he can control you, or at least put you in a very unfavorable position.

The right that was violated in this case was:

"The right not to answer a question about my personal feelings or give confidential information about myself."

Here's how that situation should have been handled by Ted:

CHUCK: Hi Ted. How are things going?

TED: Okay! What brings you down to the third floor?

CHUCK: Well, I have a concern that some of the policies of the company are not being adhered to by the guys in sales. You know, letting customers know ahead of time about price change dates so that they can buy in.

You know, I really can understand that in today's marketplace and with the squeeze in pressure for volume, how that type of thing could be happening.

To be honest with you I had some difficulty with my own people on all of the policy changes we've just gone through. Ted, what do you think is really happening in sales?

(Ted's revised response.)

TED: I really don't know. And my feelings are just that, feelings, which don't in any way influence the decisions I make.

CHUCK: Yes, but I've been honest with you. You've got to have some ideas of what is going on out in the field.

TED: Chuck, I appreciate your telling me about your concerns, but if you have them, why don't you go ask the people who really know.

How are the tentative production dates looking on our new flexible line?

There we have an O.P.E.N. Communicator recognizing a manipulative technique. Most importantly, he is understanding his rights as an individual to his own personal feelings. The result is that he did not lose control.

To provide some additional help, here are some typical manipulative techniques and the right that is being violated:

Technique	Your right
• Put the other person on the defensive immediately. Pick up something he or she did or didn't do for starters.	*You have the right not to feel guilty about actions that were taken in the past.*
• Indicate that people are taking something away from you, i.e., "Look at the position I'm in." (Implied, "because of you.") "I don't understand why you're doing this to me."	*You have the right not to accept responsibility for other people's feelings.*
• Purposely not hearing the real reason, "I almost misread what you said. Obviously, you couldn't have said..."	*You have the right not to feel guilty about the comments that you've made and you have the right to have those feelings without having to defend them.*

- To set things up so that you must come into conflict with the individual rather than with an idea or a situation: "My whole image and stature in this company are wrapped up in this fact."

  You have the right to deal only with the facts of a situation and to come into conflict only with those facts.

- To deal only in absolutes. To allow no alternatives. To force a "yes" or a "no."

  You have the right always to consider alternatives and not to be forced into a "yes" or a "no" decision.

These are but a few of the manipulative techniques and the rights which they violate. In practicing O.P.E.N. Communication, as you prepare for an interaction with somebody you perceive to be a closed communicator, be prepared to protect your rights.

You might not win in a situation with a practiced closed communicator, but you won't lose. You might not achieve what you want, but you won't lose control of yourself or your rights. If interactions with a practiced closed communicator are keeping you from achieving your life goals and ambitions, you always have an alternative. If that person is your boss, quit. If it is your spouse, get divorced.

Now that we have made that extreme statement, we must provide the most important observation about the whole process of control.

Ninety percent of the people who act like closed communicators do so not because this is their real philosophy, but because it is a routine habit learned to protect themselves against other undisciplined people.

We are all products of our experiences. Success breeds success. As we learned to communicate with other undisciplined people, we found that some defensive tactics worked. If we put other people on the defensive, we could protect ourselves. Because they seem to work, we reinforce them. The result of it all is that we have developed many habits which could be read by other people as being manipulative.

The message is, "Always give people the benefit of the doubt. Don't *assume* going into any interaction that the person is closed, selfish, and only looking out for his or her own needs."

Remember, the way he or she has acted with us in the past might be the result of what we have done to him or her.

By being consistent, by practicing with our actions the concept and structure of O.P.E.N. Communication, we will make it possible for most people to respond positively. This may not happen immediately, because we all change slowly; but if we are consistent, the positive results will happen. Remember Emerson's,

"What you do speaks so loudly I cannot hear what you say."

The great majority of people want to be open and honest in their relationships with others. They want to develop sound trust relationships. They want to achieve. Allow them the opportunity, by being a practiced, disciplined O.P.E.N. Communicator yourself.

9
POWER THROUGH COMMUNICATION

The key to power is communication. The ability to communicate opens doors that most people don't even know are there.

How many people start out with all the pieces of a master plan, with one exception — they can't communicate? The plan has no chance. Others with far less than a sure thing reap vast rewards because they can get through to people.

If, then, communication is the key to a full life, prosperity, the achievement of goals, and ultimate happiness— and it's free—why don't more people communicate effectively? It's not so difficult. Right here in these pages is everything you'll ever need to know, and there's nothing here that anyone with a grade-school education can't master. Let's review again: Why don't we communicate?

We Assume

Because we speak a language and others around us speak the same language, we assume the ability to communicate. We can ask the waitress for a cup of coffee and it's odds on we'll get a cup of coffee. We can even ask someone of the opposite sex to marry us, and if he or she has nothing else to do, he or she might agree to do it. We can tell the dog to lie down. The dog doesn't speak the language, but if it has been trained to react to those words, it will lie down.

But then come the bigger things in life ... the career path, the "once-in-a-lifetime" idea, the scheme that makes the difference between riches and poverty ... and we find a strange thing: it isn't a cup of coffee, he or she has something else to do, the dog ain't been trained. Now you need a communication effort beyond what you use every day. With it, you will succeed; without it you will fail. The reason most people fail is that they assume they understand and use the process by which people interact. They are undisciplined communicators.

The Niche

We often picture ourselves (this is part of our three-sided personality) as a certain character. There we have the making of a mistake. The character we picture assumes dimensions. A niche is formed, and we tend to operate within that niche. And, what's worse, we tend to communicate within our imagined capability. We settle a lid over ourselves. Unfortunately, the niche is easily established early in life, before we fully realize our potential. Having established the niche, we put a bridle on our image and on our aspirations.

Because human beings are innately resistant to change and fear the unknown, our tendency is to remain within the niche and operate comfortably within it. We come to understand it and feel secure inside the boundaries we have set. Our communication is geared for the niche. As time passes, we lose our ability to move out of it and onto another level.

A good communicator analyzing the expectations of a person with those pre-established boundaries can deal with that person effectively and positively. The reverse is not true. Having established the niche, one loses the capability of communicating outside the niche. He or she becomes a pawn instead of a creative person.

It would be unfair not to point out that there is nothing wrong with the niche. A lot of people live happily and comfortably within their selected strata. They avoid many of the headaches that go with higher achievement, and as a very bright English poet once said, "In the end the paths of glory lead but to the grave."

We are pointing out that if you want to get out of the niche, for whatever personal reason, the key is simply communication, and "how to do it" is in these pages.

Fear

We'll call it "fear." "Lack of confidence" is another way to put it. Often this is simply a manifestation of the "arrested development" we spoke of before. Perhaps dominant parents inhibited our communication capability when we were young, and we grew to assume that it was tough to communicate with anyone. We expected the "no" or the "turn-down"—"don't even try, it isn't going to work."

But look around. How often do you notice that effective communicators are risk-takers. They are willing to gamble. They know you've got to lose some and win some. They take the losses in stride, but because they play the game, they get good at it. The niche person who never plays the game is no match for the player. There's an old saying among top salesmen: "The sale begins when the prospect says 'no.'" There's more truth to this than fiction. A smart salesman tries to get the "no" out early in the game because when he finds out why the prospect said "no," it becomes easy to set up a win/win situation and eliminate the reason. The "no" now becomes "yes" and a sale is made. Remember, you can't win if you don't play. But as Vince Lombardi said, "Play by the *Rules* fairly and squarely."

People have said that one of the most outstanding communicators of these times is Ronald Reagan. Let's look at some of the keys to his success.

- He walked "where angels feared to tread." In every project he undertook, there was a big chance of loss and the loss would have been serious. It would affect not only his image but the course of the whole United States. But he played the game. And because he always played it and was good at it, he won.

- He was a master at win/win. He knew better than simply to ask the opposing faction to vote for him. He was a masterful leader of expectations, and when he asked for the vote, there was something meaningful in it for the other person.

- He didn't know from niche. No niche was ever established for his scope of activity. This was beyond the comprehension of even great risk-takers, and he beat them all at their own game.

Go back over the elements of O.P.E.N. Communication and compare each with Reagan's communication program. They are all there, and used masterfully—the *plan*, the *needs*, the *expectations* ... and most certainly, the *objectives*. He used them all devastatingly in a world of great communicators, and he achieved easily.

If you ask what Mr. Reagan's capabilities were beyond his ability to communicate, the answer would be—he had no capabilities beyond what many others have, and not nearly as many as most.

In recent history, we have seen the fantastic accomplishments of many people whose only tool was communication. Adolph Hitler was an Austrian paperhanger who mesmerized an entire country because he correctly analyzed their needs and expectations and shouted them from the rooftops. Franklin D. Roosevelt from a wheelchair changed the course of a nation and ultimately the world, because of his outstanding ability to communicate. Eva Peron of limited education and questionable background amassed the power of a proletariat behind her husband because of her ability to communicate. The list is long. How long would it have to be to convince our reader that none of these people used anything other than the course outlined in these pages? You don't have to have a Ph.D., a Master's, a degree in anything, or even a high school education to master the principles. We are aware that you ought to be able to read, but you don't even have to read to be a good communicator.

I personally know hundreds of people who are as successful as these leaders in their own right. They are the masters of *personal power*. They achieve up to the limit of their capacities and capabilities *and* they are happy. They have developed meaningful relationships, and are trusted and respected by their peers. They are the movers in their spheres of influence.

Each of us lives in a rather defined world...the world of our choosing. Whether you merely *exist* in that world, live in fear in that world, or control that world, depends upon the philosophy, structure, and skill of your communication capability. O.P.E.N. provides all three of those necessary ingredients.

Become a Powerful Communicator

What Does It Really Take?

1) First, the *desire:*
   - To erase the boundaries of your niche or to reign supreme within your niche.
   - To live happily and in harmony with those around you.
   - To accomplish whatever you, personally, need in order to live a fuller life.

Study the elements outlined in these pages. They aren't difficult. They are within the grasp of anyone with the capability of reading the morning newspaper or saying the Lord's Prayer.

2) *Practice*

- Try the system on little things and watch it work— with subordinates or peers, with your wife or husband, with children. Build your confidence with little things, and, unlike your school days, graduate yourself whenever you're ready.

- Make a game out of it. Games are fun, especially when you win. This game is more fun because everybody wins, and as everyone wins, you grow. Goodbye niche!

QUESTIONS AND ANSWERS

Once people are convinced that they want to develop and use the skills and structure of O.P.E.N. Communication, some additional questions arise.

The ten most asked questions are:

1. Can I use O.P.E.N. Communication if I am not the initiator of the interaction?

2. How do I know if I'm undisciplined?

3. Is everything that the "power boys" say wrong?

4. Are O.P.E.N. Communication and being a competitor inconsistent?

5. What are the key "don'ts" in using O.P.E.N. Communication?

6. Do people always know what their needs are?

7. Are there communication laws or guidelines to follow?

8. What will happen if I guess wrong at the individual's needs or experience filters?

9. Does O.P.E.N. Communication work in selling?

10. How do I get started?

The answer to each one of these questions is provided on the following pages.

Answers

1. CAN YOU USE O.P.E.N. COMMUNICATION WHEN YOU ARE NOT THE INITIATOR OF AN INTERACTION?

The answer is a definite "yes." The situation is this: You are sitting in your office and in walks a crisis. The individual immediately starts talking and the chances are that he or she has not prepared for this interaction using the discipline of O.P.E.N.

Remember, the intent of O.P.E.N. Communication is to achieve win/win. If you understand this, then both of you must first come to an agreement on what is the objective for this interaction... find the needs of both parties which will be met if we take a specific action, make sure that there are no emotional blocks right now to our achieving understanding, and that there will be some semblance of a plan for how we will go about dealing with the situation.

The way you do this when you are not the initiator is to ask questions of the other individual so that together you can define the objective and the need, identify any communication blocks, and then reach agreement.

This can be accomplished with such questions as: "So that I can understand, what is it exactly that you want me to do?"

"I think that I understand the problem that you stated. If we do take your suggestions, what will be the result and how will it benefit both of us?"

If it is obvious that the other individual is emotional and very upset, this condition has to be addressed first before any logical discussion and communication can reach a win/win. To defuse emotion, we ask questions so that the individual can talk his or her way through and get all the issues out on the table.

Most importantly, don't become defensive. Don't place the blame for the emotion on the other person. Don't try to legislate or dictate emotion out of the situation. Just listen and understand. Once the emotion is pretty well dissipated, again we can go back and ask the questions which enable both of us to determine what is the objective, what are the needs, and what plan could say "Yes, the objective can be accomplished."

2. HOW DO I KNOW IF I'M UNDISCIPLINED?

We've indicated that the undisciplined approach is even more dangerous than that of the closed communicator who is consistent.

The reason is that we confuse people with our inconsistency, which many times is read as dishonesty.

There are some indications that you were undisciplined if...

- You didn't ask the other person how he or she felt about the facts and ideas that he or she presented.
- You listened only for the facts in a situation, rather than the relationship of those facts and the feelings behind them.
- You interpreted the individual's idea internally without reconfirming that idea back to the individual through feedback.
- You did not know what you wanted others to do as a result of the meeting that you had with them.
- You did not determine in advance "what's in it" for the other person.
- You did not attempt to get any information about the previous experience of the other person.
- You reacted to a negative emotion with negative emotion ... lost control.
- You placed the blame on the other person for a misunderstanding.
- You attempted to take people's feelings away from them with logic.

- You constantly used the "big I" in our spoken and written communication.
- You played the games of "one-upsmanship" or "I've got ya!"
- You believed that the world really is out to get you, therefore you must defend yourself at all times.
- You were absolutely sure in advance how the other person was going to react and did not attempt to check out your assumption.
- You placed people in pigeon holes and didn't attempt to see any actions which might indicate that they might have moved out of those pigeon holes.
- You wanted to play it safe and avoid conflict.
- You didn't believe you had the time to do the necessary preparation for your important interactions with people.

3. IS EVERYTHING THAT THE "POWER BOYS" SAY WRONG?

In just about all of the books and articles written by the closed communicators, the authors immediately establish a paper lion or straw tiger which they then proceed to tear down.

The straw tiger is the implied assumption that the O.P.E.N. philosophy is totally against each one of the principles they identify.

This, by the way, is one of the major manipulative techniques used by the closed communicator. You establish that you and the other person or group think differently. If this is the case, then *everything* that you say is not understood or agreed to by the other party.

Now you state some universal truths. The implication is that obviously the other party does not believe those universal truths. This puts him or her in a very bad or stupid light.

Here are some of the universal truths or the "laws of survival" which the closed communicators preach, on which there is total agreement.

- *Above all else, you must believe in yourself.*

- *You must have total, utter confidence in yourself, your capacity to produce, and the fact that you have value.*

- *You must know what you want and constantly try to achieve.*

    This, in fact, is totally consistent with the O.P.E.N. approach. That's why the "O" in O.P.E.N. stands for "objective" ... to determine exactly what are your needs and what actions the other persons can take to enable you to achieve your needs.

    But with closed communicators, the implication is that if I get what I want, I have to take it away from you. This is the concept of the pie. In all interactions, there is a pie which will be divided...if I get a bigger piece, you, obviously, get a smaller one. This is not necessarily so. In fact, the real world says that each can help the other in achieving their needs.

- *You must do your homework. You must be prepared for all interactions. You can assume nothing.*

    Again, this an underlying principle behind O.P.E.N. It must be used first in preparation. Without it, you will be naive and this will set the stage for you to lose control of your own personal power.

- *You must not place too much value on anything... in fact, don't place too much value on yourself, as you relate to others.*

    Again, this is totally consistent with O.P.E.N. When an individual places too much value on any one thing, item, condition, he or she has lost control of himself or herself. An ultimatum has been laid down. There is no back-off position. A situation has been created in which the individual will, in fact, lose. If you want something so badly that you say, "I must have it at all costs," you've lost your perspective. You've lost self-control. You will lose, therefore, in the interactions with other people.

- *You must protect your rights!*

This is absolutely correct and consistent with O.P.E.N. You cannot put the burden of responsibility on the other person for protecting your rights. This is your responsibility.

We can now see that the only disagreement between the laws of the survivor and the philosophy behind O.P.E.N. is this: the survivor believes, "in accomplishing what I want, in protecting my rights, I must do so at your expense." For the O.P.E.N. Communicator, the concept that both persons receive value as a result of interactions is fundamental. There does not have to be a loser if there is a winner.

4. ARE O.P.E.N. COMMUNICATION AND BEING A COMPETITOR INCONSISTENT?

Absolutely not! Remember, there are at a minimum two types of interactions in our business life...those where the purpose is to live together with the other person in the future, and those where we're involved in a contest, e.g., where two companies are competing for a contract or a bid. It's important to remember that the contest is waged according to rules which are agreed to by all parties. These rules are supported by laws.

There are real-live contests within the same organization...for example, where two regional managers are the probable candidates for the job of Vice-President of Operations when the incumbent retires.

There are two diametrically opposed approaches to this type of situation.

One approach says, "Let me try to do everything that makes my counterpart look stupid or ridiculous." Energy is then spent in attempting to tear the other person down, rather than in attempting to insure that you will be successful by developing those skills and making those decisions which will prove to everybody that you are the right person.

Obviously, we've just stated the second approach, which is, "Don't be concerned about the other individual, but only be concerned about yourself and prove to yourself and to everyone else that you do have the capacity to handle the additional responsibility."

Does it work? Merlin Olsen tells this story about himself.

> In his second year with the Los Angeles Rams, the new rookies showed up on the field. Two of them were possible candidates to be his replacement on the first team. Both were bigger and stronger than Merlin. Merlin started to have doubts about himself and spent his time worrying about the two rookies. Finally he recognized, half-way through training camp, that there was nothing he could do about them, but there was a lot that he could do about himself. That was to play that game as professionally as he possibly could ... to commit himself totally to excellence.

> This is what he did that second year and every year for the next twelve years. As a result, he was All-Pro for fourteen years, the only man ever to achieve that honor.

5. WHAT ARE THE KEY "DON'TS" IN USING O.P.E.N. COMMUNICATION?

Here are a few of the major habits which many of us have fallen prey to, which will absolutely stop the process of gaining understanding:

- Don't assume you understand what the other person said. Feed back his or her idea and the feeling behind the idea in order to reach understanding.

- If something seems to be going wrong in your relationship with another person, don't immediately place the blame on him or her. You might be doing something which is causing him or her to become defensive.

- Don't assume or jump to conclusions. Always check out the conditions before you reach conclusions. Check out your assumptions by stating, "I think I understand how you feel."

- Don't use absolutes. These statements allow no flexibility, no alternatives. They place people in corners. This forces them to defend themselves and to reach out to attack you.

- Don't be naive. Be a professional and prepare for all interactions with people using the discipline of O.P.E.N.

- Don't evaluate the personality of an individual to his or her face. The best way to come in conflict with another person is to establish yourself as a judge over the kind of person he or she is. The best way to come in conflict with a person and to cause a defensive posture is to evaluate his or her personality. "You're lazy! You're stupid! You're not aggressive! You're not a 'go-getter!'" All of these attitudes are guaranteed to create conflict.

- Don't listen just with your ears. People communicate their *feelings* most readily by their bodily actions. Listen with your *eyes* for the feedback that individuals are providing you.

- Don't ignore silence. It is critical that we have periods of silence to allow individuals to think. Remember, the purpose of interaction is to reach understanding and then agreement. Short pauses many times can defuse the anxiety of situations. In a brief period of silence, people can start to use their minds calmly and analyze the situation, so that you can reach win/win.

- Don't ask a question without letting the other individual know why you're asking the question.

6. DO PEOPLE ALWAYS KNOW WHAT THEIR NEEDS ARE?

No. In fact, many times our needs are very vague or general.

Needs are caused by the conditions we are now living under or will be living under. If these conditions are keeping us from feeling good about ourselves or being happy, then they are identified as needs.

The O.P.E.N. Communicator should assist the individual both in understanding what are the conditions he or she is living under, and in defining his or her goals and objectives.

The professional salesperson understands that his or her first role is to assist the customer in establishing and defining the conditions under which he or she is operating. The result of this is setting priorities of needs. Once the priorities are established, the next role of the professional is to prove that he or she can provide the best answer to satisfy those needs.

7. ARE THERE COMMUNICATION LAWS OR GUIDE-LINES TO FOLLOW?

All of the following communication laws have been addressed in this book. However, here they are in summary:

- Reach for understanding before you attempt to get agreement or commitment through a course of action.

In our pressured world, so often we shortcut this process and ask for, or attempt to force people into agreement before there is understanding of:

A.   What we are really asking the person to do.

B.   What's in it for him when he does it.

There is a second dimension to this law, which says that we cannot assume that if there is understanding, agreement will follow. This is one of the major reasons why some people do not try to understand. They feel that if once they do understand, they will be committed to a course of action.

One of the most important rights we all have is the right of freedom of choice. We have a right to make the decisions that we want to make for our own reasons.

•   Our experiences give us our perception of reality.

Each one of us is a product of all of our experiences. These experiences, therefore, tell us what really is. We've lived through them; therefore, they are fact and not fantasy.

This means that you should not attempt to prove that a person's experiences are wrong. If you attempt to do this, you immediately put the other person on the defensive.

In our relationships with people we must attempt to prove that the conditions and circumstances of today are different from those which caused the individual to have the experiences of times past.

•   You can't win an argument. In an argument, the lines of demarcation are clearly drawn. The great tendency, therefore, is to attempt to prove the other person wrong. This is the definition of an argument. One person has to admit that he or she was wrong.

Even Herb Cohen in his book, YOU CAN NEGOTIATE ANYTHING says that you should never admit that you've been wrong.

You can win a debate. In a debate, the purpose is not to get the other person to agree, but to influence those who are listening and observing the debate (as in a political debate). The chances of winning your opponent over to your side are very slim.

• Power exists. Don't ignore it. Use it.

The message of this book is that power is amoral. It is a condition that exists in the world just as gravity exists. The important thing is that power is not an end, it's a means to an end. The end that we are looking for is a win/win situation. The result is that everyone that we come in contact with achieves and accomplishes up to his or her maximum capacity.

The most important element of power is our own *personal power.* This enables us never to lose control of ourselves and never to lose sight of the fact that we must achieve.

The individual with real personal power is so strong that he or she can allow others to have the same rights.

8.   WHAT WILL HAPPEN IF I GUESS WRONG AT AN INDIVIDUAL'S NEEDS OR EXPERIENCE FILTERS?

The important consideration in this answer is, "Don't say 'I know how you feel,' say, 'I think I know how you feel.'"

"Based upon our previous conversations, I'm assuming that these are the facts of the situation."

If we don't really know what the other person's needs or experiences are (and many times we don't), it is critical that we either say that we don't, or make an estimate of them based upon the information we have.

If you state your conclusions as an estimate, an assumption, then the other individual has the opportunity of either confirming or saying, "No, that is not the case," and then indicating the real facts.

9. DOES O.P.E.N. COMMUNICATION WORK IN SELLING?

O.P.E.N. Communication is the strongest possible approach in selling.

The purpose in selling (in fact, in all of our interactions with people) is to move the other person into action which will enable us to achieve what we want. Most importantly, the situation must also enable the other person to achieve his or her needs and desires. This is the win/win conclusion. This win/win conclusion is the purpose of every selling situation.

A person doesn't buy a product or a service for the sheer joy of buying it. He or she buys it to use it. That is when the person will get the *promise of performance*.

The O.P.E.N. Communication salesperson understands that his or her role is to assist the buyer in making decisions that are right for both the buyer and the seller today *and* in the future. In other words, he or she is willing to live with the buyer, with the decisions that both persons are making today, because that's how much he or she believes in those decisions.

This type of approach builds trust. Because it builds trust, it is the most powerful approach to selling.

In fact, the approach is so powerful that over a dozen times we have trained both salespeople and the purchasing agents they call on in the same room at the same time. Both need an understanding of all the concepts explained in this book. In that way, they can work together to insure a continuous relationship, a relationship where needs are met and win/win is the result.

10. HOW DO I GET STARTED?

It's simple. Make a commitment, and then establish a plan of action which will enable you to achieve that commitment.

Some of the elements of your plan could include:

1. Reread this entire book, underlining those key elements you want to remember and take action on.

2. After you've reread the book and underlined, make a separate list of the specific insights and/or actions that you want to work on. Work on them until they become habits, a part of your normal approach to communication.

3. Once you've created the list, then take one item from the list and establish what you must do in the next few days or weeks to have that item become a reality.

    For example, if you decide to concentrate on periods of silence, on slowing down your interaction with people with pauses, so that you defuse the pressure and the anxiety and enable both of you to think and, therefore, gain better understanding, take 3" x 5" cards and write the words SLOW DOWN on them. Place those cards on the mirror where you shave or put on your lipstick in the morning, in your appointment book, on your desk, on the dashboard of your car, in drawers that you open frequently during the course of the day.

4. Make a commitment to prepare for at least one major interaction a week, using the discipline of O.P.E.N. Communication. Actually write out that preparation and your 60-second opener. After the encounter is over, ask yourself the questions, "What happened? What did I do and what was the result?" Remember, practice makes perfect. In fact, the only way you can create any positive habit is to practice.

5. Share the ideas in this book. One of the best ways to remember a story or a joke is to tell it as soon as possible after you hear it. This is true in remembering anything. Therefore, share the ideas in this book with someone close to you ... a family member, a friend, an associate.

6. Tape yourself in action in specific situations. Tape a meeting that you are conducting. Tape a major presentation you're giving to a group of people. Tape some of your telephone conversations.

   Then play back the tapes, and as objectively as possible, see if your actions are consistent with what you want to do and know how to do.

These are some simple suggestions for getting started. **BUT** ... you won't get started unless you make the **commitment** to become a powerful communicator.

You've got to say to yourself, and really believe it: "THE SINGLE MOST IMPORTANT ELEMENT IN MY ACHIEVING HAPPINESS IN THIS LIFE IS MY CAPACITY TO INTERACT WITH OTHER PEOPLE. THIS IS COMMUNICATION. I BELIEVE IN THE PHILOSOPHY BEHIND O.P.E.N. COMMUNICATION. I BELIEVE THAT THE STRUCTURE CAN ALLOW THAT PHILOSOPHY TO BECOME A REALITY AND I WANT TO DEVELOP THE SKILLS OF USING THAT STRUCTURE."

Meet the Authors

William Welp, Sr.

Bill Welp is a nationally and internationally recognized expert in management education. He began his business life with 18 years experience working at the corporate management level for such companies as General Foods, Kaiser Aluminum and American Home Products. For the past 10 years, as president of T.H.E. Corporation, he has designed and executed management development programs, with the special focus of increasing sales productivity, for nearly 150 major companies, including Amstar, American Cyanamid, Ethan Allen, Union Carbide, Nabisco and Boeing Computer Sciences.

Now Mr. Welp has made his expertise available to a wider audience; this book, designed for people whose work is at home or at school as well as those who work in businesses, includes the communications techniques he presents to more than 8,000 corporate managers each year through his intensive training workshops.

Mr. Welp is on the faculty of The Young President's Organization, a course director for Advanced Management Research International, and a guest lecturer at the Harvard Business School as well as the Conference Center-Europe.

Don Scott—a self-portrait

I think I was twelve years old when I decided that communication was the name of the game; therefore, I would always be in the business of communicating.

I chose the field of business communication because I thought that was where the greatest need was. Training was a natural offshoot. We worked with universities in the development of management training, and I personally wrote a sales development program that has been used for 25 years by most of the Fortune 500 companies. I have done my management and sales training in three languages, and wrote the largest selling piece on management (800,000 copies) as well as the series in *Signature Magazine* called "Don Scott's Executive Fables."

I firmly believe that no other capability is as important in business people as the ability to communicate.

I was delighted when Bill Welp asked me to be a co-author with him on this book.